Teaching Mathematics to Deaf Children

Teaching Mathematics to Deaf Children

TEREZINHA NUNES PhD
Professor of Psychology, Oxford Brookes University
British Academy Research Reader

W
WHURR PUBLISHERS
LONDON AND PHILADELPHIA

© 2004 Whurr Publishers Ltd
First published 2004
by Whurr Publishers Ltd
19b Compton Terrace
London N1 2UN England and
325 Chestnut Street, Philadelphia PA 19106 USA

British Library Cataloguing in Publication Data

A catalogue record for this book
is available from the British Library.

ISBN 1 86156 340 X

Typeset by Adrian McLaughlin, a@microguides.net

Contents

Preface   vii

Acknowledgements   x

Conventions used for descriptions of interviews   xii

Chapter 1   Introduction   1

Is there a problem for deaf children in learning mathematics?
Does deafness cause difficulties in learning mathematics?
General processes in the development of children's
    mathematical competence
Summary and conclusions

Chapter 2   Counting and its creative uses   22

Deaf and hearing preschoolers' knowledge of numbers
Children's creative use of counting to solve sums
The signed algorithm: deaf children's own invention
Conclusion

Chapter 3   Additive reasoning: connecting addition and subtraction   50

What is at the core of additive reasoning?
Situation type 1: change problems
Situation type 2: combine problems
Situation type 3: compare problems
Summary and conclusions

Chapter 4   Reading and writing numbers   85

The logic of our number system: the concepts of units of
    different values and additive composition
Learning place-value conventions
Does the logic of additive composition really matter?

Chapter 5 Multiplicative reasoning: connecting multiplication,
             division and many other mathematical ideas   **112**

             What is at the core of multiplicative reasoning?
             A classification of multiplicative reasoning tasks
             Representing multiplicative reasoning problems
             An intervention programme for deaf children

Chapter 6 Teaching mathematics to deaf children:
             how the story began and the happy ending   **149**

             Factors related to deaf children's mathematical competence
             The assessment of our intervention programme on deaf
                children's mathematics achievement
             Conclusion

References   165
Index   173

Preface

The aim of this book is to share with parents and teachers of deaf children the results of observations and experiments that tell us about how deaf children think and learn to solve numerical problems. Parents and teachers of deaf children, and indeed deaf young people themselves, are aware of how difficult it is for the deaf to learn an oral language. However, many are often not aware that deaf children also face obstacles in learning mathematics. This book discusses the extent of the problem that deaf young people have in learning mathematics, and the causes of that problem. It also discusses how to intervene and improve deaf children's success in mathematics.

Some people believe that the connection between mathematics and language is so strong that this by itself explains why the majority of deaf youngsters have difficulties in learning mathematics. Others believe quite the opposite, that mathematics is about logic and spatial reasoning, and that the only reason deaf youngsters fall behind in mathematics is that they end up receiving a narrower curriculum and less mathematics teaching, because much more time is devoted to teaching them language and literacy. This book proposes a more refined analysis than that offered by these two extreme views. I want to illustrate this with a thought experiment.

Suppose someone asks you: 'What time is it?' What would your immediate reaction be? I expect you would look at your watch and say, for example, 'It's five past ten.' You have a *sense of time* that does not depend on your watch, and you understand the logic of time. You can tell without looking at your watch whether it is morning, afternoon or evening. You understand that today came after yesterday and that today is tomorrow's yesterday. You can tell whether you waited for a long time or for a short time for a train. But when you are asked 'What time is it?', you look at your watch, and this is what the other person expects you to do. Over the years, and through learning how to read watches, your natural sense of time developed into a more sophisticated and discriminating way of thinking and talking about time. Having a watch means being able to talk about minutes and seconds, not just morning or afternoon. Through the use of this cultural invention, the watch, you gain new measures of time and also new ways of thinking and talking about time – in a word, you gain a new way of *representing* time.

The same can be said about *number sense*. Some argue that there is an innate number sense, which is present in newborn babies and in animals. But this natural number sense is not the same one that we want children to develop in school and are expected to use throughout life. The number sense we want children to develop includes using numbers to solve problems, understanding measurement and graphs, and knowing how to use calculators and data processing software – that is, a number sense that involves mastering cultural tools and using the ways of representing number and quantity that are part and parcel of using these tools.

This example illustrates why this book has three themes. The first theme is the connection between deafness and difficulties in learning mathematics. Is this connection intrinsic to the nature of deafness? We will argue later that it is not.

The second theme is how people encode and remember information. It will be suggested that deaf and hearing people have different preferences for representing information, and do better when they use the channels they prefer. This means that, if parents and teachers learn how to present numerical information in ways that are more in tune with deaf children's preferences, the children will be able to develop their number sense better. This book offers many ideas and examples to help parents and teachers draw on deaf children's information processing strengths.

The third theme is that mathematics involves coordinating logic with mathematical conventions for representing information. So teaching mathematics to deaf children means ensuring that they coordinate their logical reasoning with counting, measuring, drawing diagrams, using number lines, and producing and reading tables and graphs. They can often solve problems through actions without being able to make the connection between mathematical representations and the logic that guides their actions. In order to help parents and teachers see how this works, the different chapters discuss the logic of number and numerical operations, and give examples of problem-solving situations that can be used to help children use logic in action and learn to combine this logic with mathematical signs.

With the invaluable help of eight teachers of the deaf, we tested a programme designed to match deaf children's information processing preferences and solve a variety of problems while learning to use mathematical conventions. The children who participated in this study made considerable progress in their mathematics learning throughout the year. We very much hope that many more deaf children will have the opportunity to benefit from this form of teaching and that parents and teachers will find that this book helps them create new ways of teaching their children.

Terezinha Nunes
June 2004

Acknowledgements

When you work on a research programme over ten years, you meet many people to whom you become indebted. There is no way you can acknowledge everyone by name. At the time I write these paragraphs, I relive an amazing set of experiences and think of the many friends and collaborators who were part of my life during these investigations.

Constanza Moreno, a student, a research assistant, a joyful friend, was there all the time. She taped the first mathematics lessons to deaf children I ever observed. She became curious with me about why the children had difficulty and what could be done to promote their learning. She did a master's dissertation and a doctoral thesis while working on this research programme. She learned to sign and encouraged me to do the same. Constanza was a good observer and a committed researcher. The studies would not have been the same without her.

The teachers of the deaf, the children, and the headteachers in the schools where the work was carried out were fantastic. Imagine what it means to have researchers coming in and out, year after year, and to accommodate them in terms of time and space, scheduling interviews with children, classroom observations, assessments, teachers' meetings and intervention sessions. I am very grateful to them all for their dedication, patience and continuous support. The schools that participated in this project were: Grove House School for Deaf Children, Heathlands School for Deaf Children, Culloden Primary School, Darrick Wood Junior School, Kingsley Primary School, Knollmead Primary School, Norwood Green Primary School, Laycock Primary School and Sellingcourt Primary School.

Other friends came onto the scene as I tried to learn and think about deaf children. Ursula Pretzlik, Jenny Olsson and Diana Burman had questions and their own observations to contribute. Howard and Jacqueline Swinbourne patiently taught me BSL and put up with my limited short-term memory for visually and simultaneously presented information.

They created a learning environment where I did not feel impaired, though I could not process and retain information presented in sign as well as they could. They never complained and always thought my mistakes were funny rather than stupid. Peter, Daniel and Julia, my family, put up with the late suppers that resulted from my being an evening student of BSL. Anna Brett patiently read the manuscript and edited it. I am thankful for her support and help.

I am especially indebted also to the institutions that supported this work, which would not have been possible without their generous help. The Nuffield Foundation provided the resources for the different investigations reported in this book. Their contribution goes beyond these material resources and included advice at different stages of this process and also positive responses, which are invaluable when you know, as a researcher, that there are no easy answers. The British Academy supported me through a Research Readership so that I could have the time to write this book – what a great privilege! – while pursuing other endeavours related to investigating children's difficulty in learning mathematics. And last but not least, I want to acknowledge the support I have found at the London Institute of Education and Oxford Brookes University, where there is an unambiguous commitment to research and to researchers' personal development.

None of these friends and institutions can be held responsible for my views, right or wrong. Without their support, though, I would have no views on deaf children's mathematics learning. Without them, the deaf children who benefited from the intervention described in this book would not have had the chance to see mathematics learning as such a positive experience and to improve so much in their achievement. They can be considered responsible for providing this learning opportunity to the deaf children.

Finally, I want to thank Clare Gallaway, who read the manuscript and made several helpful suggestions. She wrote critical and positive comments, which were very much appreciated. I hope future readers will read it as carefully as she did.

Conventions used for descriptions of interviews

...   Indicates that a non-relevant section of the speaker's comments was not included.

( )   Describes actions by the speaker.

[ ]   Explanation inserted by author to facilitate comprehension of the interaction.

CHAPTER 1

Introduction

Throughout the many years that I have worked with children and watched them learning mathematics and solving problems, I have never ceased to be amazed by the fascination that most children have for solving problems. When I observe them solving problems outside the classroom, no matter how difficult these might be, most children try very hard to make sense of the problem and to find a solution. The solution might not be right, but it is invariably reasonable from the child's viewpoint.

Once, a lively 8-year-old boy and I had just finished a problem-solving session, where he was tackling difficult multiplication problems in a teaching experiment, and we saw the headteacher as we walked to his classroom. 'Miss, I have been doing some really hard maths,' he said with a grin. It was the end of the day, and I came back to the room to collect my materials and leave. The headteacher was waiting for me. She was curious about what I had been doing in the experiment; the boy I had been working with was considered very weak in maths. He had, in fact, started the session showing signs of fear and stress. When I gave him the first problem, which should have been quite simple, he gave me an answer right away, a number, clearly without having had any time to think the problem through. But the teaching experiment I was trying out was not about giving numerical answers, but about showing through actions how to solve the problem. So I didn't have to say to him that it was not the right answer. I just had to pose new questions to him, which helped him see a path to the solution. When he completed the first exercise, he gave me the grin he later gave to the headteacher, relaxed, and said that this was actually fun. Anyone who has succeeded in solving a problem that seemed very hard to begin with can empathize with this boy: actually, succeeding in intellectual tasks is fun.

Working with deaf children solving mathematics problems has been no different. Once they become involved in problem-solving, they too experience the joy of intellectual success. So why write a book about teaching mathematics to *deaf* children? Is it not like teaching mathematics to hearing children? It is certainly easy to see why language learning is different for deaf and hearing children and perhaps even to extend the same reasoning to understand why literacy learning has to be more difficult for deaf than for hearing children. But why mathematics?

This book analyses different aspects of mathematics learning: why we need to consider deaf children's strengths and difficulties above and beyond the expected difficulties that mathematics learning causes to all children. Much of the evidence discussed here is based on research with hearing children and analyses what is difficult for all children in mathematics learning. Concepts that are difficult for hearing children are also difficult for deaf children. But there are special considerations when teaching mathematics to deaf children. They relate both to the role of language in mathematics teaching and learning and to the preferences for cognitive processing that deaf children have, some of which differ from hearing children's preferences. It is hoped that at the end of this work you will find that you can see the children's viewpoint, although it should be recognized that much more research is needed for a thorough understanding of how best to teach mathematics to deaf children.

This introduction starts by analysing whether there is a specific problem for deaf children in learning mathematics and why this problem might exist. The research described in this first section is quantitative, in order to assess the size of the problem. The second half of the chapter presents a theoretical analysis of processes involved in children's mathematics learning, and selects specific issues that might make teaching mathematics to deaf children different from teaching hearing children. The subsequent chapters in this book analyse core mathematics concepts, their difficulties for all children, and the specific challenges that could be faced by deaf children. In each chapter, the analysis is followed by a description of successful attempts to find a better path for teaching those concepts to deaf children.

Is there a problem for deaf children in learning mathematics?

Educators in the UK have for a long time been monitoring the attainments of deaf children in mathematics. A report by the National Council of Teachers of the Deaf, published in 1957, compared the performance of 246 deaf pupils in four special schools in England with the standardized norms for hearing pupils. The pupils' progress in mathematics was assessed through the Schonell Arithmetic Test, which contained two assessments of arithmetic. The Schonell Arithmetic Test is standardized to produce an arithmetic age: for the average child the arithmetic age should be the same as the chronological age, though a small difference between the chronological and the arithmetic ages is often observed in either direction. The average arithmetic age for the deaf pupils was two and a half years below their chronological age. This means that, for example, a 10-year-old would be performing in arithmetic similarly to a child aged between 7 and 8 years. This large difference between the chronological age and the arithmetic age does give cause for concern.

About a decade later, Wollman (1965) tested approximately one-third of the pupils from 13 schools for the deaf in the UK and a comparison group of 162 hearing pupils in secondary schools. Deaf pupils were once again found to perform significantly worse than the hearing cohorts. Wollman's study does not describe the arithmetic age of the pupils, as in the study by the National Council of Teachers of the Deaf, but makes a comparison between the means for the hearing and for the deaf pupils. In order to understand this comparison, it is necessary to think about how means work in describing a group.

A mean for a large group of pupils is normally at the middle of the distribution of scores: many pupils have a score that is the same as the mean, some will have higher and some will have lower scores. For most large groups and age-appropriate tests, it is possible to estimate how many pupils will score within a certain range above and below the mean. This estimation allows us to understand the significance of the difference between a child's score, for example, and the mean. The statistic that is used to help us understand the importance of a difference between a particular score and the mean is the *standard deviation*. For most groups, about two-thirds of the pupils will have scores in the range between one standard deviation below and one standard deviation above the mean. If a child's score is more than one standard deviation below the mean, this places the child roughly among the weakest 15% of the group. For all practical purposes, this means that this child needs help. In Wollman's study, the average for the deaf pupils in the mathematics test was about one standard deviation below the mean for the hearing pupils. This indicates that about 50% of the deaf pupils' performance was equivalent to that of the weakest 15% of the hearing pupils. These comparisons give us an idea of the size of the problem.

But it is not only the quantitative aspect that gives cause for concern in the results of the study by Wollman. An analysis of where the deaf pupils succeeded and failed gives further reason for concern. It was found that a large proportion of pupils showed a skill in simple arithmetical processes; far more errors were attributable to lack of understanding than to mistakes in calculation. Thus the deaf pupils were learning how to carry out sums but not when to use them to solve problems. This is not an unusual difficulty for hearing pupils (see, for example, Brown, 1981; Bryant, 1985) but it was clearly a more serious obstacle for the deaf pupils.

Hine (1970) also found a considerable delay in mathematics age in a study of 104 deaf pupils. The delay for 10-year-olds was about 2 years but the delay for 15-year-olds was more serious: deaf 15-year-olds on average showed a competence comparable to that of hearing peers aged 10 to 11 years.

Unfortunately, the situation was much the same another decade later. Wood, Wood and Howarth (1983) carried out a survey, including 80 schools in England and Wales, on a group of 414 hearing-impaired pupils and a comparison group of 465 hearing pupils in secondary school. They used the Vernon and Miller Graded Arithmetic Test (Vernon and Miller, 1976), which they thought would have little contamination of reading difficulties. The hearing-impaired youngsters were about three and a half years behind the hearing pupils. Thus an average deaf school leaver would show a mathematical competence equivalent to that of a hearing pupil at age 12 to 13 years. This bleak result, which is even worse than that of the initial study by the National Council of the Teachers of the Deaf, does not mean that deaf pupils' mathematics achievement is getting worse over time. The tests used in the two studies are very different and the Vernon and Miller Test does require reading instructions in order to solve many of the items.

More recently, we (Nunes and Moreno, 1998a) compared the performance of 85 deaf pupils with the norms for the NFER-Nelson 7–11 series of mathematics assessments. The pupils were in Years 2 through to 5 (aged between 8 and 11 years) in special schools and mainstream schools with units for the hearing impaired in eight different schools in London. None of them had additional difficulties beyond the hearing loss. The mean for the deaf pupils was two standard deviations below the mean for the hearing pupils; this is equivalent to saying that the mean score for the deaf pupils was comparable to the result for the weakest 2% of hearing students. This very poor average performance was influenced by the fact that some of the deaf pupils had extremely low scores, which we included in the calculation of the mean. We then excluded from the calculation of the mean the 16 pupils whose score was so low that it was below the bottom 2% for their year group, and recalculated the mean. The result was an average score for the deaf pupils that was roughly one standard deviation below the mean for hearing pupils, and thus comparable to the weakest 15% of the hearing pupils.

Finally, the recent norming of the Stanford Achievement Test for deaf and hard-of-hearing students carried out in the USA (Traxler, 2000) confirms this bleak picture once again. In order to avoid giving students assessments that were too difficult and thus would prove frustrating, Traxler did not administer the grade-appropriate level assessment to all the participants but gave them assessments that were judged appropriate on the basis of an initial screening. Well over half of the students aged 9 or older and as many as 90% of the 15-year-olds were given tests that were appropriate for hearing pupils at grades lower than their own. This by itself suggests an educational delay. The two mathematics tests administered, Problem Solving and Procedures, showed results that were similar in one way: the growth curves for the deaf and hard-of-hearing students are much flatter than those for hearing students. In Problem Solving, 80% of the students at age 14 showed a level of performance considered basic or below basic knowledge of mathematics problem-solving. In Procedures, 80% showed a level of performance that was considered below basic at the same age level. Thus very few deaf and hard-of-hearing students in the USA seem to be attaining a sound level of mathematics knowledge according to the Stanford Achievement Test.

The picture is therefore not an encouraging one. Deaf pupils' mathematics achievement has been documented as very weak for about five decades of research and there is no indication that educational changes that may have benefited hearing children's mathematics learning have succeeded in closing the gap between hearing and deaf pupils. This bleak picture cannot be taken lightly. Mathematics is a gate-keeper into many courses at university, where the minimum achievement is a grade C in the standardized examinations at age 16 (currently, GCSE). Numeracy tests are also given routinely in selection procedures for employment. Failure in mathematics is not an option: it is urgent that we reach a better understanding of why deaf pupils are not making better progress in mathematics, and how to change this situation.

The different shades of grey

Before proceeding any further, it is important to say that the picture of deaf children's mathematics achievement is not uniform, and that looking at means does not tell the whole story. In every study, there is variation between pupils, and in every study there are deaf pupils who perform at average and above-average levels for their age. In the study by Wood and colleagues (1983), 15% of the profoundly deaf pupils showed scores equal to the average for the hearing students or better.

Frostad (1996), in a study in Norway, observed a higher percentage of deaf students performing at average levels or better (37.5%) even though the average attainment was still significantly lower than that for hearing students. This figure was reported for all levels of deafness and it cannot be directly compared to the results described by Wood and colleagues, because different tests were used. Though better than the results observed by Wood and colleagues, these results are still an indication of difficulties for the deaf pupils, because in a standardized test 50% of the sample who participated in the development of the test norms performed at the average level or better.

In our own work, we have also found variation. As indicated earlier, 16 of the 85 children – about 19% – had scores that were so low that they were not included in the table for conversion of raw scores into standardized scores. In order to scrutinize the distribution of the scores more carefully, we looked at the percentage of children in different bands of standardized scores. The test we used was standardized to produce a mean score of 100. Considering only the children who were severely or profoundly deaf, the results were: 25% were in the band below a standardized score of 50 (equivalent to about the weakest 2% of the hearing group); 8% were in the 51-to-70 band (which is at about the weakest 5% of the hearing group); 31% had standardized scores between 71 and 90 (corresponding to the weakest 40% for the hearing norms) and the remaining 36% had standardized scores of 90 or above (which were at average or above for the hearing group). Our results, obtained with English pupils much younger than those who participated in the study by Wood and colleagues, are more similar to the results observed by Frostad. But, as indicated earlier on, there is no possibility of direct comparison across the studies, owing to the use of different tests.

In short, the three studies show that there is no uniform picture for the mathematics attainment of all deaf pupils. There is among deaf pupils, just as there is among hearing pupils, variation in success. Unfortunately the results show that the skies are not blue, but different shades of grey.

Does deafness cause difficulties in learning mathematics?

By now you must be wondering whether deaf children have difficulties in mathematics exactly *because* they are deaf. Some people argue that mathematics is a form of language and, because learning languages is difficult for deaf pupils, they find learning mathematics difficult. This argument would see a direct, and thus inevitable, connection between deafness and mathematics learning difficulty. Is this argument sound? What evidence is there to support this idea of a direct causal connection between deafness and difficulty in learning mathematics?

First, let us consider whether the argument is sound. The first part of the argument is that mathematics is a language *and* that it is thus difficult for deaf pupils because they find learning languages difficult. Both parts of this argument can be questioned.

Many people would argue that mathematics is not simply a language. Mathematics is a way of representing the world and communicating about number and space – and in this sense it could be considered as a language – but it involves more than that. Learning mathematics involves learning specific ways of thinking about number and space, and using these to process information. This discussion, though, is fruitless for our investigation of why deaf pupils find mathematics difficult. Whether it is a language or not, in a way it does not matter, because the second part of the argument is certainly flawed.

It is simply not true that deaf children have difficulty in learning languages. Deaf children of deaf parents, who sign to them from the time they are born, learn sign language as ably as hearing children learn oral language (Goldin-Meadow, 2003). Their vocabulary growth and mastery of the grammar of sign language are comparable to that of hearing children (Lillo-Martin, 1999; Newport and Meier, 1985; Petitto, 2000). Sign languages assume all the functions of spoken languages and are used not only to communicate about the here-and-now but also about worlds that are not present (Goldin-Meadow, 2003). Signs are not direct representations of objects or actions but are conventions, and just like spoken languages have to be learned.

The misconception that learning languages is difficult for deaf children comes from the fact that most deaf children – about 90% – are born to hearing parents, who do not know a signed language. Therefore there is a mismatch between the parents' knowledge and the children's language learning ability. The parents' input of a spoken language, which the child cannot receive, is as much beyond the reach of the deaf child as ultrasounds are to the human ear. The mismatch often continues for a long time, as many parents do not find out that their child is deaf until well into the child's second year of life, when the child does not show the expected production of spoken words. And when they do find out, they would themselves need time to learn sign language, if this is the type of education they choose for their child. Thankfully, this delay in diagnosis may soon be one less obstacle for deaf children because of the systematic introduction of diagnostic procedures early in the infant's life.

Thus it is now clear that deaf children do not have an inherent difficulty in learning languages but that the mismatch between the verbal input produced by hearing parents and the child's sensory abilities results in language delay. It should then be clear also that the idea that deafness causes difficulties in learning mathematics because of the very nature of mathematics and the very condition of deafness can be rejected.

However, is it possible that there is an indirect causal connection between deafness and difficulty in learning mathematics, perhaps because spoken language is an essential part of how mathematics must be learned? What type of evidence would support the idea that there is a causal connection between deafness and mathematics learning? Different possibilities are considered in the sections that follow.

Correlational studies

One way in which psychologists investigate whether there is a causal connection between two human characteristics – in this case, deafness and mathematics difficulty – is to analyse whether it is possible to show a statistical relation between the two. If deafness causes mathematics difficulty, the level of hearing loss should be related to the level of difficulty. In most studies, finding that there is a mathematical relation between the two characteristics does not directly support the causal relationship between the two, but rather provides evidence that there *could* be a causal connection. The reason for a careful conclusion – that is, saying that there could be a causal connection – is that different possibilities exist to explain a mathematical relation between two characteristics. One is that the first characteristic causes the second: in this case, deafness causes mathematical difficulty. The second possibility is that the causal connection goes the other way around: in this case, mathematics difficulty causes deafness – a possible but very unlikely explanation of why there is a mathematical relation between deafness and mathematics difficulty. The third possibility is, nevertheless, plausible: that both characteristics are caused by a third factor, i.e. deafness and mathematics difficulty could both result from a third characteristic such as damage in brain functioning. In this case, the cause of deafness, and not the level of deafness, might show a connection with mathematics difficulty. Deafness is sometimes a genetic condition, which may or may not be associated with learning difficulties or other problems. Deafness might also be acquired, for example through meningitis, and the illness could cause other problems besides deafness.

Three of the studies referred to earlier on, which investigated the mathematics achievement of deaf pupils, also analysed the connection between the level of deafness and mathematics achievement. In order to investigate whether there is a statistical connection between two characteristics, correlations between them are calculated. Correlations vary between –1, when there is a perfect correspondence between the two characteristics but an inverse one (as in this case, the greater the deafness, the smaller the mathematics competence), and +1; a correlation around 0 signifies that there is no statistical relationship between the two characteristics. Wollman (1965) found no correlation between the level of deafness and mathematics achievement. Wood and his colleagues (1983) found a weak negative correlation between the level of deafness and the mathematics achievement, close to –0.3, which indicates a feeble statistical relation between deafness and mathematical achievement. We (Nunes and Moreno, 1998a) did not find a statistical relation between deafness and mathematics achievement. Thus, three independent studies, which included a total of more than 500 deaf pupils, failed to provide evidence for a causal connection between level of hearing loss and mathematics competence. The hypothesis of a direct causal connection between deafness and mathematics competence thus becomes less plausible.

What if most types of deafness were not related to mathematics achievement, but there was a third factor, causing both deafness and mathematics difficulty? There is little research that can help answer this question. One of the difficulties in carrying out this type of investigation is that in a very large proportion of deaf children there is no identified cause of deafness: there is no family history of deafness, there is no birth trauma, no illness (such as meningitis, ear infection or prenatal German measles) nor genetic syndrome that explains why the child is deaf. In our study, this was true for just under 50% of the children. We found no association between cause of deafness and mathematics achievement, but our sample of children with a known cause of deafness was very small – 43 children – and the number of children with the same cause of deafness was thus even more reduced. With such small samples, it is not possible to find a connection between type of deafness and mathematics difficulty.

We can, however, follow this argument to its consequences to see what could be learned if a study showed that some types of deafness have a direct causal connection to mathematics difficulty. Let us suppose that it was in fact found that a particular cause of deafness – I will call it deafness type A – was definitely caused by some form of brain dysfunction that also caused difficulties is mathematics. This study would explain why children who have deafness type A have difficulty in learning mathematics, but not why the majority of deaf children show such difficulty. So, finding a connection between one type of deafness and mathematics difficulty does not help us understand the plight of the majority of the deaf pupils.

The only clue that could be found in the literature was a large review of the research on deafness and intellectual development. If deafness were to result in lower levels of intelligence, this would result, in turn, in lower mathematics achievement, because research has shown abundantly that there is a relationship between intellectual level and achievement in mathematics. Braden (1992, 1994) carried out a systematic, quantitative analysis of the results of different studies on the relationship between deafness and intelligence. He carefully considered the nature of the tests given – whether they involved verbal or non-verbal reasoning – as well as other important factors that would affect the validity of the study, such as the number of participants, the methods of delivery of the tests and data analysis, and whether the cause of deafness had been known and analysed. Verbal reasoning skills require children to solve problems and display knowledge that involves language. For example, a verbal problem-solving task might involve analogical reasoning. In a verbal, semantic analogy task a child could be given a pair of words that have a particular meaning relation between them – for example, 'milk' and 'cheese'; the child is then given a third word, say 'leather', and asked to provide the fourth word. In order to give a correct answer, the child would have to consider that 'cheese is made from milk' and provide a word that shows the same relation to 'leather' – e.g. shoes or handbag. A non-verbal reasoning problem might be solving a puzzle, such as assembling a picture of a car from a number of pieces, or completing a picture where the discrete elements have a particular relationship to each other. Figure 1.1 provides an example.

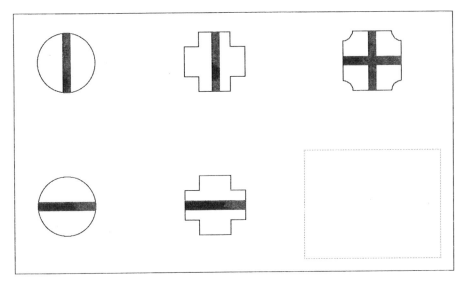

Figure 1.1 An example of visual analogy. What figure should be drawn into the rectangle?

Because there is a correlation between vocabulary knowledge and verbal reasoning tasks, it should come as no surprise if deaf people perform poorly on verbal reasoning tasks. But an analysis of verbal tasks is meaningless when comparisons between hearing and deaf people are made, because verbal tasks are clearly not 'fair tests'. There is typically some correlation between verbal and non-verbal reasoning because some of the cognitive operations that are involved in the tasks may be the same – Figure 1.1 shows that it is possible to use the cognitive operation of making analogies with both verbal and non-verbal materials. In spite of this correlation and the difficulties that deaf people might have in solving verbal problems, there is no reason to expect that deaf people would be at a disadvantage in non-verbal reasoning tasks.

Braden concluded from his extensive review of studies that there is no evidence for a deficit in non-verbal reasoning skills among deaf people whose deafness is caused by identified genetic causes and who have no other impairment than deafness. When deafness is caused by illnesses that may have negative effects on the brain, there may be intellectual loss, though this is not a universal consequence.

This research is highly relevant to the question of a connection between deafness and mathematical ability. It has long been established that non-verbal reasoning is strongly correlated with mathematical ability. Braden's analysis thus leaves us with a puzzle. If deaf children have the intellectual ability to learn mathematics, what is getting in their way?

In order to consider possible answers to this question, it is necessary to think about how hearing children develop their mathematical competence and then ask to what extent the developmental processes involved could explain deaf children's difficulties. In the remaining section of this chapter some basic ideas about the development of mathematical competence are considered. The essence of the argument to be presented is that different mathematical concepts pose specific difficulties for all children learning mathematics. In each of the chapters that follows, a mathematical concept is considered and the specific difficulties that it poses for children are analysed. The pieces of the puzzle of what is getting in the way of deaf children's mathematics learning will be identified throughout the chapters. The concluding chapter will aim at putting the picture together.

General processes in the development of children's mathematical competence

Some preliminary thoughts

Let me start this section with an imagined situation. Suppose I ask you: What is eight times nine? How do you get the answer? Most hearing people who have attended school will have memorized this number fact. They know the verbal string 'eight times nine, seventy-two'. The fact that we know the answer to this problem as a memorized verbal string is seen as compelling evidence that oral language is an integral part of our knowledge of mathematics. This could lead us to think that deaf children have some difficulty in learning mathematics because they find it hard to memorize verbal strings.

Imagine a second situation. Suppose I gave you this story problem: 'Mary bought eight bars of chocolate. Each bar cost 9p. How much do the chocolate bars cost altogether?' What would you have to do to solve this story problem? Many people would answer that one would first have to identify the correct operation, multiplication, and then find the answer to what is eight times nine, in order to answer the question. This second example suggests that people have to identify a correct operation (is it addition, subtraction, multiplication or division?) and they apply it to the numbers to solve this problem.

Researchers and teachers have for a long time thought that solving story problems – and, by extension, solving mathematics problems in practical situations in everyday life – involves two steps. The first is to understand the description of the problem and identify the correct operation. The second is to carry out the operation. Both of these steps are seen as involving language. It is suggested that, in order to construct an interpretation of the situation, we need language. It is argued that this is so even if we were to go to a shop, for example, take the eight bars of chocolate from a box and see the price, 9p, written on them. In this practical situation, much as in the story problem, we would need to say to ourselves: 'Eight bars of chocolate at 9p each: that means eight times nine'. This description is intuitively appealing – reading it, we might think that this is the way *everyone* solves such problems. I will argue that there is some truth in this description for some of us, but that for most of us some aspects of this description are incorrect, even if they appear to be true.

There is little doubt that in order to solve a problem, even if it is a practical problem such as the one in the shop, we need to construct a *mental* representation of the situation. After all, we solve problems by thought operations, and our thinking works with mental representations. It also seems intuitively right that if we construct an incorrect mental representation of the problem, we are more likely to produce a wrong than a right answer. So we have to construct an adequate mental representation for the problem. But the idea that we then have to proceed to identify *the correct operation* is not supported by research. For many mathematical problems, including the story problem above, there is more than one logical way to find the answer. Coming up with eight times nine is only one way, though probably the preferred way for people who went to school and memorized the times table.

Much research with people who work in markets shows that this is not the preferred way for unschooled people. People solving practical problems in everyday life use different procedures, which depend on the number system that they use and on the procedures commonly adopted in their culture.

Gay and Cole (1967) were the pioneers of this line of investigation. They observed how the Kpelle, an indigenous group in Liberia, solved arithmetic problems. Their indigenous counting system, which they use to talk about and represent numbers, was not used to construct and memorize multiplication tables. Thus if they were asked to solve multiplication problems, their normal procedure for obtaining an answer was to use stones or fingers to represent the numbers and count. If asked how many chickens a man was selling, if he had three chickens in each of two baskets, the Kpelle would either count 3 two times on their fingers or make two groups of three pebbles and count them. Gay and Cole's work in Liberia brought home the message that multiplication tables are procedures, and that different procedures can be used to solve the same problem. One procedure is to create a representation of the numbers and count. Of course this is a tedious and error-prone procedure, particularly when the numbers are large. It is perhaps not appropriate for our society, where large numbers are quite common, but it is nevertheless correct.

Many years later, working with children in Brazilian street markets, we (Nunes, Schliemann and Carraher, 1993) had the opportunity to extend Gay and Cole's observations and produce new findings that helped us understand better the difference between a problem-solving procedure and the logic of the problem. In order to simplify the description of this work, the example given here is about a multiplication story, but it should be remembered that this is a general argument, which is not confined to multiplication problems.

We asked children who had different levels of experience in street markets to solve a series of arithmetic problems. In one example, we asked a youngster in third grade, JG,[1] who would have been taught the written computation procedure for multiplication, how much we would have to pay if he were selling a toy car for 50 *cruzados* (the Brazilian currency at the time) and we bought 15 toy cars. He did not write down the sum 15 × 50, as he had learned to do in school. Instead, he counted in fifties as he pointed to his fingers in one hand: 'fifty, one hundred, one fifty, two hundred, two fifty'. He then paused, repeated 'two fifty', then said: 'five hundred.' Next he returned to the pointing to fingers and counting procedure: 'five fifty, six hundred, six fifty, seven hundred, seven fifty', and gave 'seven hundred fifty' as the answer. JG's procedure is an extension of the counting procedure observed among the Kpelle, but it is more efficient because it combines addition of equal groups with counting in

---

[1] In the Brazilian school system there is often a large variation in age levels within the same grade because children may start school later than the expected age of 7 or be retained for failure, most often in reading. Although the expected age of a child in the third year of school is 9, JG was 10 years old.

larger units. He counts in units of fifty, five times, then doubles that – obtaining the answer to 10×50 – then adds to this another lot of five fifties, and reaches the right answer. His procedure, which we termed *repeated groupings*, is different from recalling the answer from a multiplication table and also from calculating it in writing.

Counting, calculating with repeated groupings, and carrying out a multiplication sum are different procedures for solving problems, but none of these procedures is the essence of problem-solving. What makes the different procedures work is that they are all under the control of a logical understanding of the situation. Counting works for the Kpelle in the problem described earlier only if they construct two groups of three pebbles. If they were to construct one group of three pebbles when they hear that 'the man had three chickens in his baskets' and a second group of two pebbles when they hear that 'he had two baskets', and then count the pebbles, they would come up with the wrong answer. The logic is used in the choice of how to represent the numbers in the problem: making two groups of three pebbles is not a simple matching of pebbles to number words but represents a choice stemming from the understanding of how to represent the problem.

The same is true of the repeated grouping procedure: it works because it is under the control of a logical interpretation of the situation. JG established a system of correspondences. For each toy car, represented by a finger, he counted one fifty. When he reached five fifties, he doubled this and knew that two times five fifties is the same as ten fifties. Finally, he set correspondences between fingers and fifties until he reached 15 fifties. This analysis, and other examples presented later in the chapter about multiplicative reasoning, show that what is essential to the logic of multiplicative situations is the systematic correspondence illustrated in JG's procedure. Any procedure that preserves this correspondence will lead to the correct answer.

A theory that says that, in order to solve a story or a practical problem, it is necessary first to identify the correct operation and then to implement the calculation, leads to the prediction that children must make more mistakes when solving story and practical problems than when solving sums, because the former two (solving story problems and practical problems) would require solving the sum plus another additional step, which could also lead to error. The results of our research with Brazilian children (Nunes, Schliemann and Carraher, 1993) show without doubt that solving specific arithmetic operations is not the only path to solving school-type story problems or practical problems that come up in everyday life. We compared the children's ability to solve sums with their ability to solve school-type story problems and their ability to solve practical problems. The questions were comparable across conditions. For example, one sum used was 35×10. The equivalent story problem was: 'There are 35 children in each Year 1 class in a school. There are 10 Year 1 classes. How many children are in Year 1 in this school?' The equivalent practical problem was: The youngster interviewed was selling coconuts for 35 *cruzados* each; we said we wanted 10 coconuts and asked how much we would have to pay. The rate of correct response in these different conditions of testing was: 37% correct responses to arithmetic operations; 74% correct responses to school-type story problems; and 98% correct responses in the practical situation. These rates of correct responses are not consistent with the theory that children need to interpret the problem, and identify and implement the correct operation to succeed in problem-solving.

Thus, it is concluded that the idea that children have to represent the meaning of the situation and find *the right operation* is misguided. They have to understand the situation and find a procedure that is in line with the logic of the situation. This procedure in multiplicative situations may involve counting in ones, counting in larger units and repeated additions or multiplications.

Unfortunately, the idea that children must interpret a *verbal* description of situations and then identify *the correct operation* in order to solve arithmetic problems has resulted in misguided teaching approaches. One example is the method that suggests that children should be taught to identify 'key words' in story problems and, through these, identify the correct operation. Teachers who work with key words will produce lists of words that are connected to a particular operation; for example, the word 'altogether' is identified with addition and the words 'less' and 'fewer' are identified with subtraction. However, it is now quite well established that this method of teaching interferes with, rather than promotes, good reasoning in story problems. Think of the problem: 'Pete has three apples. Ann also has some apples. Pete and Ann have nine apples altogether. How many apples does Ann have?' If a child were to add upon seeing the word 'altogether', the answer would be wrong. Vershaffel and De Corte (1997) have shown that this problem does lead to a large number of wrong answers based on addition. If the problem is presented to the children with a different language, where the key word method works, the number of correct answers goes up. The alternative language that they describe is: 'There are nine apples. Three of them belong to Pete. The rest belong to Ann. How many apples does Ann have?' The fact that the children succeed when the problem is presented with a different language is not evidence in favour of the key word method: it actually shows that, if children are encouraged to base their representation of the problem on isolated words, they cannot become good problem-solvers. Teaching children to connect particular words to particular sums cannot work, because there are many different ways to talk about the same situation.

To sum up, this section started out by considering a common belief about how people solve arithmetic problems. According to this commonly held view, when we encounter an arithmetic problem in everyday life or as a story problem in school, we first need to understand the problem and identify the correct arithmetic operation. Then we need to calculate the sum. This view of how we solve problems is partially right: it is true that we need to construct a logically sound representation of the problem. But it is also partially wrong: once a sound logical representation has been constructed, there are many different procedures to reach the correct answer – there is not just one correct arithmetic operation.

Why should this perhaps subtle point matter? It matters a lot, because it is an important indicator of what we want to teach children so that they become good problem-solvers in mathematics. If it were correct that we need to teach them to identify *the right procedure*, our teaching would focus on procedures. However, if it is true that we need to teach children to construct sound logical representations of situations, our aim has to be to work with children's logic. These are two radically different pathways, even if in the second case we might also teach children about procedures.

In the next section a theory of how children develop their mathematical reasoning is presented. This theory guides the design of the activities for teaching deaf pupils that are discussed in the later chapters.

A theory of mathematical concepts for teaching mathematics

The connection between learning mathematics and logic will not come as a surprise to any readers of this book. The point about the central importance of logic for mathematical competence was made more than half a century ago by Jean Piaget (see, for example, Piaget, 1952), but it is probably made also by many unnamed teachers numerous times to their students in the classroom. It is easy to recognize that mathematical reasoning is a form of logical reasoning. This section suggests that this is true but that it is not the whole story. The framework used here is inspired by the work of the French psychologist, Gérard Vergnaud, who was one of Piaget's students. Vergnaud built on Piaget's conception of the use of logical reasoning in mathematics and brought other insights to the analysis of mathematical concepts. Vergnaud (1997) suggests that mathematical concepts – and thus teaching and learning mathematics – involve three dimensions to be mastered. Children need to understand the logic of the concept, the signs used in mathematics to talk and think about the concept (which can be linguistic but can also be numeric, algebraic, graphic, schematic drawings etc.), and the situations in which the concept is used.

To expand on the first idea, let us consider why *logic* is important even for the simplest mathematical task, counting. In order to count correctly, children have to establish a correspondence between each object counted and the number words. This means counting all objects once and only once. They also have to understand that the last word they say when they count indicates the number of objects. The work of psychologists like Gelman and Gallistel (1978) suggests that at the age of 4 many children already understand these counting principles. They seem to be worse at doing the counting – that is, implementing the procedure themselves – than at checking whether someone else has done it correctly. In order to count correctly, they have to remember the counting words and simultaneously make sure that they are pointing at every object once and only once; under these circumstances, they may actually skip some or count some objects twice. However, when they watch someone else, they can check that the procedure is correct without the burden of execution (much like backseat drivers do!). Gelman and Meck (1983, 1986) and later Briars and Siegler (1984) asked children in the age range 3 to 5 years to say whether a puppet, manipulated by the experimenter, had counted the objects in a row 'OK or not'. The puppet sometimes obeyed the counting principles and sometimes made mistakes. In both studies it was found that the children could judge correctly whether a puppet had counted OK or not, and that the children did better in this task than when they themselves did the counting. If the puppet skipped an object or counted the same object twice, they knew a mistake had been made, though they might have made the same type of mistake themselves, inadvertently, when counting. They also knew that the puppet had made a mistake if the puppet did not indicate the last number counted as the number of objects in the row. These interesting experiments with such young children show that even the simplest activity – counting to know how many objects – requires logic, and that even in such simple problems there is a difference between logic and carrying out a procedure.

But logic is not all, even for counting. When we count, we put a *sign* for the number in correspondence with an object. The sign can be a word – one, two, three etc. – or a gesture, in the case of a sign language. In either case, we need to create a representation for the object within a counting system. It is possible to reason about quantities without using signs to represent numbers. Much of Piaget's work focused on this logic of quantities without the use of number signs. For example, in one of his tasks, Piaget (1952) asked children to place a marble into a jar at the same time as he himself placed a marble into another jar. The jars had different shapes: one was thinner than the other. After having placed many marbles into the jars, the level reached by the marbles in the two jars differed: it went up higher in the thinner jar. Piaget then verified that the children remembered that they had placed a marble into their jar for every marble that he placed in his. Then he asked the children whether the number of marbles in the two jars was the same. Many children could answer this question correctly on the basis of logic, because they knew that there was a one-to-one correspondence between the jars. But they could not know how many marbles were in each of the jars because they had not counted. Thus, Piaget argued, there is no need to count in order to understand number.

Piaget is, of course, right: not all mathematical problems depend on our knowing the exact numbers in order to find the answer. But he overlooked another side of mathematical reasoning, one which involves arithmetic: in order to solve arithmetic problems, we do need to know the numbers. When we solve an arithmetic problem – say, a part–whole problem like the one about Pete's and Ann's apples presented in the previous section – we must understand its logic. In this case, the number of the whole – that is, how many apples Pete and Ann have altogether – is exactly the sum of the parts. But this is not sufficient to answer how many apples Ann has. It is also necessary to use signs for numbers – words or signed numbers – to be able to find the numerical answer. Thus, whenever we need to answer numerical problems, we need to know a number system, understand the conventions for number representation it involves, and how to manipulate it. Because mathematical signs are conventions, they have to be learned. So learning mathematical signs is an essential element in the development of children's mathematical competence. In the later chapters of this book the significance of different mathematical conventions will be discussed.

In the same way that it is possible to use different procedures to solve the same problem, there are also different mathematical conventions for representing mathematical information. Counting can be carried out in words in different languages, which are different conventions, and it can also be carried out in sign. There is now much evidence, which will be reviewed in the next chapter, that some counting systems are easier to learn than others. Think of the multiplication story problem presented earlier on; it was presented in words. The same information can be represented in visual form, with a small tag attached to each of eight chocolate bars. The information could also be presented in a table, where the number of chocolate bars would be placed in correspondence with the price of the chocolate. The research that will be reviewed later will show that the way in which information is presented to children does have an influence on how well they can solve problems. The critical point is that, in order for children to solve arithmetic problems and succeed in mathematics, they must be able to represent numerical information and to manipulate these numerical representations. In order to succeed in school and later in the community and in their jobs, they must learn to use the systems of signs that are used to represent numerical information in school and in job settings. So mathematical concepts and reasoning involve not only logic; they also involve systems of signs used to solve problems and used in communication about numerical information.

The third dimension to be considered in the analysis of mathematical reasoning is the understanding of situations in which the reasoning is applicable. Piaget (1952) often used the example of transitive reasoning to explain the importance of situations for logic. If you know that stick A is longer than stick B, which in turn is longer than stick C, you can conclude that A is longer than C. This is an example of transitive reasoning. But not all relations are transitive, like the relation 'longer than'. The relation 'father of' is not transitive: if Paul is the father of John and John is the father of Mary, you must not conclude that Paul is the father of Mary. This is not a transitive relation.

This example seems so obvious that it may be necessary to consider others. Here, only one further example will be given, because every chapter that follows will consider the situations that relate to the logical ideas in the chapter. The relation 'equal to' is transitive but the relation 'different from' is not. If Jasmine has the same number of balloons as Julia and Julia has the same number of balloons as Deborah, we conclude with certainty that Jasmine and Deborah have the same number of balloons. But if all we know is that Jasmine does not have the same number of balloons as Julia and that Julia does not have the same number of balloons as Deborah, we do not know how Jasmine's and Deborah's balloon collections compare. They might have different numbers, but they might have the same number of balloons.

Piaget used these examples to argue that, even if logical principles were innate and programmed in the brain, as some have argued (e.g. Wynn, 1992; Geary, 1994), there is still an important role for experience in the development of mathematical competence. He argued that only experience with situations allowed children to understand the logic of the situations. This must be borne in mind later, when we discuss the situations in which children learn. Some researchers (e.g. Furth, 1971) have argued that deaf children suffer from a lack of experience in different situations. For example, it has been found that deaf children have a delay in the development of money concepts in comparison with same-aged hearing children (Austin, 1975). This delay could perhaps be due to the fact that hearing children can go out to shops and buy things on their own whereas the deaf children are less likely to do so because of the difficulties they might face when trying to communicate with the shop assistants.

What, then, if experience with money were shown to be important for children? This would place deaf children at a disadvantage, and other learning opportunities might have to be created to replace those missed in everyday life.

In summary, mathematical concepts involve *logic, systems of signs to represent the concept*, and *situations* where the concept is used, which help us understand the concept. All children might face difficulties with the logic, the systems of signs, and the understanding of the situations in which particular logical principles can be applied. The question examined in the subsequent chapters is whether the difficulties posed by these three dimensions of the concepts might be greater for deaf children than for hearing children. In order to answer this question, and identify the pieces of the puzzle, each of the dimensions will be considered.

Summary and conclusions

A review of results obtained by deaf pupils in mathematics achievement tests, considering data from a very large number of pupils over five decades and in different countries, suggests that deaf children do show weaker performance in mathematics than hearing children. This weaker performance is observed both in arithmetic and in problem-solving. However, this weak performance is not homogeneous: some deaf pupils (estimations vary between about 15% and 35%) perform as well as their hearing peers in mathematics.

The studies reviewed indicate that the reasons for this difficulty are not yet clear. It does not seem to be likely that deafness directly causes difficulties in mathematics learning. This direct causal link is not compatible with several observations. First, some profoundly deaf pupils perform well enough in mathematics tests. Second, there is no correlation or only a very weak correlation between level of hearing loss and mathematics achievement. Third, there is no evidence for a connection between causes of deafness and difficulties in mathematics. Fourth, deaf pupils' average performance in non-verbal intelligence tests is not below the norms for hearing pupils, and non-verbal intelligence tests are highly correlated with mathematics learning.

These results suggest that deaf children's difficulties are not inevitable but that they are at risk for developing mathematics difficulties. In order to understand the nature of this risk, it is necessary to consider how children solve problems and learn mathematics: what is difficult for all children and what could be especially difficult for deaf children.

A common view of how children solve mathematics problems is that they need first to interpret a problem verbally, then choose the correct operation to solve the problem, then implement this operation – either through remembering verbally memorized number facts or through written computation procedures. This theory of arithmetic problem-solving is inconsistent with research results. It is clear that this theory does not make a distinction between the mathematical logic of problems and the procedures used to solve them. Research has shown that the same problem might be solved through the use of different procedures that all represent the logic of the situation.

An alternative description of mathematical competence was provided by the French psychologist, Gérard Vergnaud, who suggested that there are three aspects of mathematical competence that must be considered, both in research and in teaching children. The three aspects are the logic of the problem, the systems of signs used to think and talk about the problem, and the situations in which the logical principles can be validly used. All three aspects are mastered through experience and learning. So each of the chapters that follow in this book will be concerned with how children learn to use mathematical signs in different situations in order to solve problems.

A final word is required about the description of studies where the participants were deaf, before moving on to the next chapter. Many studies in the literature do not provide detailed information on the levels of hearing loss of the participants or the language used in the education, spoken or signed. So this information is often not presented. Sometimes it may also be omitted to avoid lengthy descriptions of samples. Descriptions of our own studies include this information but the information is not repeated when the same participants' results on different tasks are presented in different chapters. Readers wishing to obtain more information on participants of studies by other researchers are advised to consult the original work (full references are provided at the end of the book).

CHAPTER 2
Counting and its creative uses

Some researchers (Gallistel and Gelman, 1992; Dehaene, 1997) have suggested that young children have a pre-verbal sense of numerosity that can be used to recognize small numerosities, up to three or four, rapidly and accurately. This claim has even been extended to the ability to carry out addition and subtraction (Wynn, 1992) though this latter assertion is disputed by recent research (Houde, 1997; Wakeley, Rivera and Langer, 2000). As impressive as infants' ability to recognize small numerosities may be, infants' ability is of little relevance to this analysis of the development of children's mathematical competence. Though some researchers believe that this innate sense of numerosity is the basis for the later developing number system that uses counting (Butterworth, 1999), it is recognized that the early number sense displayed by infants is neither learned nor much affected by practice (Dehaene, 1997). Because the focus of this book is on what can be taught and changed through learning, this chapter is concerned with another system for representing number, which develops later and relies on more explicit representations of number – especially counting.

Counting allows for the representation of any numerosity with accuracy: as argued in the preceding chapter, a counting system is necessary for providing answers to arithmetic problems. This chapter considers the development of counting skills in hearing and deaf children – what is difficult for both groups of children – and the creative use that they make of counting later on when solving arithmetic problems. Their later use of counting is termed *creative* because the evidence suggests that children develop these uses of counting without instruction: they are, therefore, their own invention.

Zarfaty, Nunes and Bryant (2004) argued that a good way to start the search for the causes of deaf children's mathematical difficulties is to find out when deaf children first begin to fall behind their hearing peers in mathematics. One possibility is that deaf children fall behind hearing children before they start school. They might be behind in their logical reasoning, their ability to mentally represent and remember numbers, or their ability to count and use counting to solve problems. If deaf preschoolers already show significant difficulty with mathematics learning, it is likely that they would profit less from school instruction than hearing children. A second possibility is that they start school with the same logical reasoning and understanding of situations that hearing children have. They may be just as capable as hearing children in counting and solving problems through counting, but the curriculum they encounter and the teaching methods that are used in school may not be as suited to deaf as to hearing children. So knowing when deaf children begin to do worse than hearing children at mathematics should place us in a better position to understand what causes their difficulties.

This chapter is organized in three sections. In the first section, deaf and hearing preschoolers' ability to represent numbers and to count is analysed. In the second section, hearing and deaf children's creative use of counting to solve sums is considered. The last section describes a specific discovery by deaf children: the signed algorithm.

Deaf and hearing preschoolers' knowledge of numbers

If a teacher is asked whether her pupils, say in the first year of school, know something about multiplication, she might very well answer: 'No, I haven't taught that yet.' For many people, in order for children to know something in mathematics, they have to be taught. Thus it comes as a surprise to many parents – a very pleasant surprise, actually – and also to many teachers that children can have much mathematical knowledge without having been exposed to formal school teaching. However, there is quite good consensus among researchers (see Ginsburg, Klein and Starkey, 1998) that preschool children construct much *informal* mathematical knowledge before they start to learn arithmetic in school and that this informal knowledge is necessary for children to be successful in learning the *formal* knowledge that is transmitted in school. 'Informal knowledge is grounded in problem-solving situations with concrete objects, and children construct it through their interactions with the physical and social world. In contrast, formal knowledge entails the manipulation of a system of written symbols, and children typically acquire this type of mathematical knowledge in school' (Ginsburg et al., 1998: 413). In this section two types of informal knowledge of number are examined: children's recall of number and counting.

Number recall

Psychologists have used a variety of tasks to assess the informal mathematical knowledge of children in the age range 3 to 5 years. An essential consideration in developing these tasks, which distinguishes them from those used with infants, is that they are not *recognition* but *recall* tasks. The difference between recognition and recall is assumed to be a matter of the mental representation necessary for performing the tasks. An everyday experience with the difference between recognition and recall, familiar to most of us, relates to memory for faces. We may meet someone at a party and remember meeting the person but be unable to remember what the person looked like. However, if we happen to bump into the same person, say sometime during that week, we might recognize the person. In order to remember the person we need to build a mental representation that we can evoke; recognition memory does not require building such a representation.

Piaget (1952) pioneered the use of tasks to assess young children's knowledge of number. One of the simplest tasks he designed was a number copying task, in which he showed the children different displays with certain numbers of counters (e.g. 4, 8, 6 etc.). The children were asked to place on the table the same number of counters, sometimes in the presence of the array to be copied, sometimes in its absence. Reproducing the number of objects in an array in the absence of a model is a recall task: it is necessary to have a mental representation of the number in order to obtain an exact copy. Saxe, Guberman and Gearhart (1987) used this task extensively to investigate differences in children's informal mathematical knowledge at an early age and mothers' teaching styles, when the mothers were asked to help the children solve the tasks. They analysed the demands of this task and concluded that it involves three steps: recognizing that it is necessary to count in order to reproduce the number, counting the objects in the model, and counting the objects in the reproduction. Mothers who were effective in teaching their children how to solve this task were able both to recognize which steps might be missing when the child attempted to solve the problem and ensure that the child performed each of them.

We (Zarfaty, Nunes and Bryant, 2004) thought this was a good way to start the investigation of whether deaf children are already behind their hearing peers in informal mathematical knowledge at ages 3 and 4, so we designed an experiment where we compared hearing and deaf 3- and 4-year-old children in a number reproduction task. The first question we had to consider when setting up this comparison was how the model to be copied should be presented to the children. Previous research indicates that the way in which items are presented influences children's ability to remember them – and that this influences how well deaf children do in comparison with hearing children. We thus needed to design fair and also relevant tests for the comparison between deaf and hearing children.

What do we know about deaf and hearing people that helps design these fair comparisons? Since the pioneering work of Conrad (1979) and Hermelin and O'Connor (O'Connor and Hermelin, 1972; Hermelin and O'Connor, 1975), it has become clear that there are differences between deaf and hearing people's coding strategies in short-term memory tasks, which in turn affect what they remember. Short-term memory tasks typically involve presenting a number of items to people and asking them to recall the items. One of the differences between deaf and hearing people is that deaf people have a preference for coding the information in these tasks visually whereas hearing people have a preference for using language to code the information – a strategy named *phonological coding*, because it is based on sound. These differences are picked up from the types of errors that people make when remembering the items. Suppose that the task was to remember a list of capital letters, and that the letter X was among the items. Mistakes made by deaf people in recalling this letter typically include visually similar letters, such as K, M or N. Hearing people's mistakes in recalling the letter X include letters whose name is similar, such as F or S. Thus the difference between using preferentially visual or verbal codes has an impact on what is remembered (or mistakenly remembered, in this example).

The use of visual and phonological codes also seems to influence how things are remembered. Phonological codes are more useful in preserving the order of the items; visual codes are more useful to preserve the location of the items. This means that there are memory tasks where deaf people are better than hearing people and other memory tasks where deaf people are worse, depending on how the information is presented – spatially or sequentially – and how it is to be recalled. Marschark and Mayer (1998) have produced an assessment of findings in this domain, so a review is not presented here.

However, to make the point more clearly, a study by Todman and Seedhouse (1994) is considered because their task is both relevant and fair. They compared deaf and hearing schoolchildren on a memory task originally designed by Pascual-Leone (1970) to assess a cognitive ability – rule learning – which he thought was very closely related to mathematics learning. In this task, the children are asked to learn an action response to an arbitrarily paired visual cue: for example, if a square with a purple background is presented, the child has to open the mouth. The task is rather complex and there are a number of pairings between the figures and responses to be learned. Once the children have learned the pairs, their memory can be tested using either a spatial or a sequential presentation. In the spatial presentation, they are shown a matrix with four figures; the matrix is then covered and they are required to perform the four actions that were paired with the figures. In the sequential presentation, they are shown the figures one at a time, and after the series is completed they are required to perform the actions. In the sequential presentation, recall may be required in the same order as the figures appeared (*serial recall*) or in any order (*free recall*). Todman and Seedhouse observed that the deaf children were superior to the hearing children in the task where the figures had been presented simultaneously in the spatial display. Thus they were better able to encode the spatially presented information and then produce the associated actions. The sequential presentation produced different results for the serial and the free recall. The hearing children were better than the deaf children in the serial recall condition but there was no difference between the deaf and the hearing children in the free recall condition. In short, the way in which the items were presented – spatially or in a temporal sequence – and the way in which they had to be recalled – serial or free recall – affected the children's performance. The deaf children had an advantage when the presentation was spatial and were at a disadvantage when the presentation was sequential and recall was serial. Marschark (1993) has shown that this disadvantage of deaf people with serial recall does not appear in all experiments: it is only manifested if the number of items to be recalled is large, and thus puts high demands on memory.

Numbers are used to count both spatially and sequentially presented objects or events. For example, a child may want to know how many marbles he/she has, and these may all be available for counting at the same time. It is just as likely that a child is asked to count, for example, how many times he/she threw the ball in a game. So we (Zarfaty, Nunes and Bryant, 2004) decided that it was important to use both spatial and sequential presentation of items in our number reproduction task.

Twenty children – ten deaf and ten hearing – participated in our study. The mean age of the children in both groups was about 39 months. Nine of the deaf children were profoundly deaf; one was moderately deaf. Eight of the profoundly deaf children had cochlear implants. The deaf children were being educated orally in mainstream nurseries but also attended a nursery school for deaf children at least twice a week. We gave the children 24 number reproduction tasks, where the number of items in the display varied between 2 and 4: in 12 of these the display was presented spatially and in the other 12 it was presented sequentially. In the spatial presentation, the children saw a row of blocks on a computer screen, and these were then put into a box. In half of the trials, the blocks simply appeared on the screen simultaneously and then moved into the box; in the other half, the children saw a puppet making the row and then putting the blocks into a box (also presented on a computer screen using a video). In the temporal, sequential presentation, the blocks appeared and then disappeared into the box one at a time. For half of the trials the puppet opened her hand, showing a block on her palm, and then placed the block into the box; for the other half of the trials, the blocks simply appeared on the screen and then disappeared into the box through animation. Next to the computer were 20 blocks and a box identical to the one seen on the screen. Once the children had observed the display on the computer, they were asked to do the same thing with the blocks. They had no difficulty in understanding this instruction and placed blocks into the box. The latter variation – the presence of the puppet versus the use of animation – made the task more interesting for the children but had no effect on their performance. The number of items in the display did not affect the children's performance either: on average, they were just as accurate with 2, 3 and 4 blocks.

The task was of moderate difficulty for both groups of children. There were six trials in each of the different conditions, and the mean number of trials in which the children reproduced the correct number of blocks was 2.2 in the condition where they had the least amount of success, and 5.1 in the condition where they had the best results. The deaf children were correct significantly more often than the hearing children when the displays were presented spatially, and this is where the best performance in the experiment was observed. Contrary to what we expected, there was no difference between the deaf and hearing children when the blocks were presented sequentially. This may be explained by the fact that the number of items was small and that recall in this experiment is more similar to free than to serial recall.

These results are very positive. They tell us that the deaf children are not inherently poor in number representation, regardless of whether the presentation of the items is spatial or sequential. They also tell us that they are actually better than hearing children when the number presentation is spatial. Because this was observed at such an early age, it is possible that deaf children's superiority in spatial tasks may be connected to their need to adapt to a world where visual cues have to be used to a greater extent than in the world of hearing children, who can rely on both visual and sound information. Our results, along with those observed by Todman and Seedhouse (1994), suggest that there may exist a general superiority among the deaf in processing visual information, in comparison to hearing children. It has been suggested that the superiority of deaf people in some visual tasks is connected to their knowledge of sign language (see, for example, Emmorey, 1998). Though this may be true of some tasks, it is not true of all: neither the children in our study nor those in the Todman and Seedhouse study were signers. Thus visual processing seems to be a strength in deaf children's cognitive abilities, and it should be picked up by educators when designing instruction for deaf pupils.

Knowledge of the counting string

Counting objects, it was already argued in Chapter 1, is not simply a matter of learning number words but also involves logic: there must be a one-to-one correspondence between number words and objects and it is necessary to understand that the last number represents the number for the whole set. But what about learning number words? What could be difficult about it?

In order to count correctly, the number words must be learned in a sequence. This is a task that requires serial recall – which, by now, we know is an activity that is more difficult for the deaf than for hearing people when there is a need to remember a large number of items. In the case of counting, hearing as well as deaf people would find learning impossible if the number string had no order to it. Imagine the task of counting one thousand objects: to count a thousand objects, you need to be able to reproduce one thousand words in the same order, a task that would be unconquerable by deaf or hearing people if there were no connection between the number words.

Over the course of history, most cultures have developed counting systems that make it unnecessary to memorize the number words one by one. Because systems have rules for generating the number labels, learners can actually generate number labels that are higher in the string than the particular words they learned. In English, the counting system is organized around tens and its multiples, but some numbers in the system are irregular. The units – one to nine – are basic number labels, which combined with the labels for decades form new number labels. So we have twenty-one, twenty-two, twenty-three etc. up to the next decade, thirty, which combines again with the units up to the next decade, and so on. If the system were completely regular, the word for *eleven* should be ten-one, *twelve* should be ten-two etc. Some counting systems – such as those used in Japanese and Chinese – are regular in this way. Other systems – like English, Spanish and Portuguese – show some irregularities, but these are confined to smaller numbers. Thus the task of learning to count in English involves two processes: serial recall of number labels up to nineteen and then the use of rules for combining decades with units, then hundreds with decades and units, then thousands with hundreds, decades and units, and so on.

Much research has described how children learn the counting string in different languages. Ginsburg (1977) and Fuson (1988), working with US

children, identified several cues in children's counting that help us understand the difficulty of the task of learning the counting string and the
processes that eventually help children master it. One of the cues used in
identifying learning processes is the type of error made in different parts
of the counting string. In the first part of the string, formed by the number labels that have to be memorized – namely, the units and the labels in
the first decade – children make mistakes such as omission of one or more
words (e.g. 11, 12, 14), reversals (13, 15, 14, 16) and repetitions (10, 11,
12, 13, 11, 12, 14). They may reach a point in the middle of the decade –
e.g. 13 – and then say they have no idea what comes next. In contrast,
once they reach twenty and the subsequent decades, children make considerably fewer mistakes within a decade and many more mistakes going
across the decades (e.g. 39, 50, 51, 52). Also, they are much less likely to
stop counting in the middle of a decade than at the end. This type of error
analysis suggests that children learn, at least implicitly, the rules that guide
the formation of number labels, and use these rules in order to produce
the counting string.

Grégoire and Van Niewenhoven (1995) report similar results for learning to count in Belgian French and point out another type of mistake,
phonological confusions. For example, having said 'treize' (13), the child
might go on to 'dix-sept' (17) – owing to the phonological similarity
between 'treize' and 'seize' (16).

Finally, the analysis of how far the children can count also reveals the
rule-governed nature of learning to count. Miller and Stigler (1987)
observed that the point at which young preschool children stopped
counting – in their study, children aged between 4 and 5 years in the USA
– did not reflect a slow and continuous acquisition of items one by one.
Within the first two decades – that is, in numbers up to 20 – the stopping
point might have been at a random point in the string. However, if the
children reached 21, it became less likely that they would stop anywhere:
when they reached a decade, they were unlikely to stop counting within
that decade. Thus the most likely point would be at the decade combined
with 9, for the children who did not know the subsequent decade. Finally,
they observed that almost all the children who could count up to 60 could
count to 99. This large increase in the children's knowledge of the counting string – an increase of about 40 items – suggests that the children had
now mastered the rules for formation of decade names as well as their
combination with units.

What is it like for deaf children to learn the counting string? There are,
of course, two specific answers to this question. One relates to learning
the oral counting string, the other relates to learning to count in sign. But
there is also a common aspect between the two: the fact that learning the
counting string is a serial recall task involving many items leads to the

prediction that it should be more difficult for deaf than for hearing children to learn to count.

Learning the *oral counting string* is not as simple for deaf children as it is for hearing children. This should be expected because learning to count requires serial recall of phonological items: the number *words* must be recalled in a fixed order. We (Nunes and Moreno, 1998a) found that many deaf children in their second and third years in primary school were still not able to count to 60. This sample included deaf children educated orally in BSL (British Sign Language) and in SSE (Sign Supported English), and the majority of the children were either severely or profoundly deaf (for a more detailed description of the sample, see Chapter 3). This performance compares poorly to hearing children's knowledge of the counting string: the majority can count to 60 by the end of their first year in school. Some of the deaf children showed phonological confusion errors, going from, for example, 16, 17, 18, to 81, 82 etc., an error type that we did not observe in hearing children in primary school. Even some children in Year 4 could still not count to 60. Thus a considerable delay in learning the counting string was observed when the children were learning to count in English. Nunes and Moreno suggested that teachers of the deaf could place greater emphasis in learning to count, because lack of knowledge of the counting string limited the children's ability to solve numerical problems.

Learning to count in BSL – British Sign Language – is similar in some ways and different in others from learning to count in English. BSL shows regional variations in counting but some of the principles across these variations are the same. This discussion concentrates on one system, described in Figure 2.1.

Numbers in BSL, like numbers in English, also require two learning processes: there is a simple, rote memory process involved in learning some signs whereas other signs can be learned with the support of rules. However, BSL relies more on rule-based learning than English does. The numbers 1 to 5 (see Figure 2.1) are formed by keeping the hand upright, the palm towards the signer, and extending the fingers in an ordered fashion, starting with the index, moving across to the small finger, and then the thumb; all five fingers extended indicates the number 5. The number 6 starts a new rule: 6 is signed with the hand in horizontal orientation and the thumb extended; the remaining fingers are then extended to sign numbers up to 9. The number 10 starts a new series. There are different ways of signing number 10 – with both hands showing 5, with a special sign, or as shown in Figure 2.1, by signing 1 and then 0 to the left of the 1. Numbers 11 and 12 are irregular but, from 13 to 19, numbers are signed in the same way as in the units, but are associated with a waving movement in the horizontal or vertical direction. The direction is determined by the

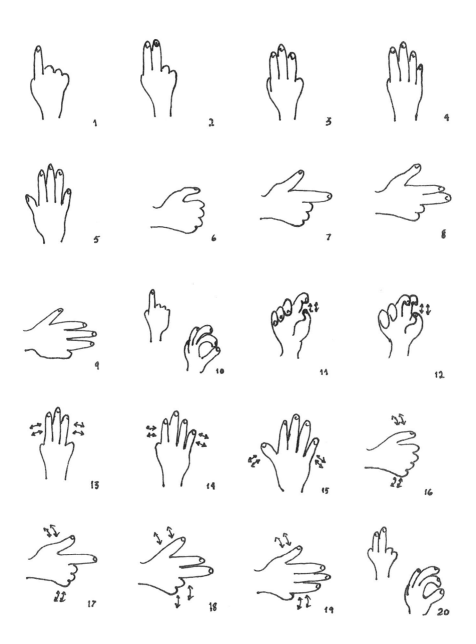

Figure 2.1 Counting in British Sign Language (BSL).

way the number is signed: 3 is signed with the hand upright so the waving movement to indicate 13 is left and right; 6 is signed with the hand in horizontal orientation so the waving movement to indicate 16 is up and down.

There are regional variations for signing numbers in the teens. From 20 onwards, a new set of rules of combination applies: 20 is signed as 2 and 0, with a spatial displacement indicating the same organization as in writing, 2 to the left of 0; numbers 21 to 99 follow the same rule. It should be remarked that the direction of signing (2 to the left of 0) is the opposite of the direction as perceived when the observer faces the signer. This is actually always the case in sign languages. This means that there is a spatial rotation when perceiving in comparison to signing numbers.

The reliance on more rules in BSL (and other sign languages, such as French, Belgian French and Spanish sign languages) than in English should make it easier for deaf children to learn to count in sign than in English, because the number of items to be recalled without the support of rules is smaller in BSL than in English. Whereas the English counting string requires memorizing 19 number labels without the support of rules, BSL numbers use rules from the start. This prediction of greater ease of learning to count in BSL, however, would only hold if young deaf children find it easy to learn rules. If deaf children found it difficult to learn rules, there would be no simplification of the serial recall task by breaking the string to be memorized into smaller, rule-based segments.

Blank and Bridger (1966) hypothesized that learning rules requires verbal processes that allow for rehearsing the rule internally. If this hypothesis were correct, learning to count in sign would pose great difficulty for young children because of the need to learn many rules. They carried out two experiments where they compared the ability of young deaf and hearing children to learn arbitrary rules in an experimental task. The children were aged 3 and 4 years in one experiment and 5 and 6 years in the second experiment. They found no difference between the deaf and hearing children in three of the four comparisons they made; in the fourth comparison, where the rule to be learned was based on tactile material, the deaf 5- and 6-year-olds performed better than the same-age hearing children. Thus Blank and Bridger concluded that there is no evidence to suggest that young deaf children are worse at learning rules than hearing children. The results from this experiment suggest that, though signed numbers require learning a greater number of rules, there is no reason to expect that deaf children will find the system difficult to learn.

This greater reliance on rule organization leads to an interesting prediction: that deaf children should perform well in tasks where they are asked 'What number comes after x?' if x is a number within the rule-based sequence. Their performance may even be better than that of hearing children if the same question is not within a rule-based sequence for hearing children. For example, if asked 'What number comes after 7?', deaf children should be at an advantage because 8 is generated by the same rules that generate 7 in sign whereas for hearing children there is no rule connecting 7 and 8. If this prediction is correct, it will bring further evidence in support of the idea that rule learning is not more difficult for deaf than for hearing children. The interest of this task is that it reveals a flexible use of the counting string: some children can count but cannot answer this type of question because they seem to know the number labels as a rigid sequence and cannot start anywhere. A second task that is used to investigate the flexibility of children's knowledge of the counting string is to ask them to count backwards. It is assumed that a rigid knowledge of counting is not sufficient to allow children to count backwards.

In summary, the analysis of learning to count in BSL indicates that learning the counting string, even though facilitated by the use of more rules, is likely to be difficult for deaf children owing to the serial recall nature of the task. Although it may be easier to learn to count in BSL than in English, deaf children may still need more time to learn to count than hearing children. However, within the portions of the string they have learned, deaf children may show greater flexibility in their knowledge, and may be able to answer questions that hearing children cannot answer, like 'What comes after x?'.

Learning the counting string

Two studies have considered deaf children's learning of signed numbers in comparison to hearing children's learning of the counting system in their own languages: one analysed American Sign Language (Secada, 1984) and the second, Belgian French Sign Language (Leybaert and Van Cutsem, 2002). The structure of both systems is similar to BSL, with a double base organization of the counting string around 5 and 10. Both studies showed that deaf children in preschool have counting strings that are shorter than those of hearing children in the same grade and age level – i.e. when they are asked to count as high as they can, deaf children count up to a number that is smaller than the number reached by hearing children. In the study by Leybaert and Van Cutsem, the children were compared not with their age cohorts but with children in the same year of school. The consequence is that the deaf children were on average one year older than the hearing children. Though they had the same amount of preschool experience, they were still behind in counting. These results reinforce the expectation that serial recall tasks are more difficult for deaf than for hearing children.

Leybaert and Van Cutsem suggested that it is possible that deaf children lack experience in counting up to higher numbers in preschool. The teaching groups are typically smaller for deaf than for hearing children. Preschool teachers often ask the children to count how many children have come to school or how many are taking part in an activity. Because the groups are smaller in deaf classes, the children will have fewer opportunities to count up to larger numbers.

Finally, Leybaert and Van Cutsem report an interesting analysis of where the children stopped counting – that is, at what number they said that they did not know what comes next, even though the researcher encouraged them to go on. Because of the greater use of rules of composition in signed numbers than in oral numbers, it was expected that the deaf children would stop more frequently at the numbers where there is a change of rules. This was actually the case: nine children stopped after 5 or 15 whereas the remaining four stopped at other points in the counting string where the rule could still be applied. This indicates that the majority of the deaf children were taking advantage of the rules that organize their counting system and facilitate recall. Even so, serial recall is still more difficult for them than it is for the hearing children.

To conclude: deaf children do show a delay in learning the counting string. This delay is not likely to be explained by a difficulty in learning rules – young deaf children are as good as hearing children in learning rules, and their learning of the counting string provides evidence that they are using rules to remember the numbers. The delay may be a direct consequence of the serial recall nature of the task or a result of lack of experience. Whether this delay in learning to count is a result of lack of experience or a result of the serial recall nature of the task, the implication is that teachers of the deaf should devote more time to teaching the counting string than teachers in preschools for hearing children do.

Flexibility of knowledge of the counting string

Secada (1984) and Leybaert and Van Cutsem (2002) also asked the children in their studies the question 'What number comes after x?'. In order to compare the deaf and hearing children, they placed the children in groups of equivalent counting ranges: it would not be a fair comparison if a child who can count to 30 were to be compared with another who can only count to 6, for example. This procedure is called matching; we say that the children were *matched for their counting range*. The comparison of deaf and hearing preschoolers' ability to answer the question 'What comes after x?', when they were matched for counting range, showed that the deaf children were better at answering this question. The deaf children were also better at counting backwards. These two tasks are used to indicate the flexibility of the children's knowledge of the counting string. These positive results thus suggest that, once the deaf children learn the counting string, they are quite flexible in their use of this knowledge.

The study of children's learning of the counting string helps us move forward a little in our understanding of what could and what could not be an explanation for deaf children's difficulties in mathematics. Counting strings have to be learned. They are a very important aspect of mathematical knowledge because we use numbers to represent quantities and solve arithmetic problems. They are an example of serial recall tasks; that is, the order of the items in the counting string must be preserved. Because of deaf children's greater difficulty with serial recall tasks, learning the counting string is difficult for them. However, once they have mastered this learning task, they are better in the flexible use of the string than hearing children of similar knowledge of counting. Though the comparison is with younger hearing children, it is quite important. If the result showed that the deaf children were less flexible than the hearing children matched for knowledge of counting, this would suggest that practice in counting might not help the deaf preschoolers. This positive result should provide greater incentive for a more systematic teaching of counting to deaf preschoolers.

Counting objects

The studies by Secada (1984), Nunes and Moreno (1998a) and Leybaert and Van Cutsem (2002) considered deaf children's ability to count objects – that is, to coordinate the counting string with the logic of one-to-one correspondence and indicate the number of objects in the set. All three studies show that deaf and hearing children's performances when counting objects within their counting range are very similar. It would not be a fair comparison to consider sets that require the children to use number signs that they do not know. Thus, as with the results described in the preceding paragraphs, the comparison of deaf and hearing children's ability to count objects suggests that the main obstacle for the deaf children in preschool is learning the counting string.

Nunes and Moreno (1997) have, however, identified a difficulty in the implementation of the one-to-one correspondence procedure among deaf children who sign. When hearing children count, they speak and point to the objects to keep track of the correspondence. If they are prevented from pointing and have to rely only on the correspondence between their gaze and each object, their performance deteriorates (Alibali and DiRusso, 1999). When hearing people learn to sign, they often sign the numbers with one hand and point to the objects with the other. They create a model of counting for deaf children which is based on their own preference for sequential information: point to an object, sign a number afterwards. Although we did not collect information about this in a systematic manner, we observed that deaf children who counted in this way – pointing with one hand and signing the number with the other – tended to become confused: had they already counted this object or not? They often stopped and counted again, slowly. Other deaf children combined the sign for the number with the pointing gesture: the hand signed 1 as it pointed to the first object, signed 2 as it pointed to the second object and so on. These children seemed more skilled and more at ease with counting.

We do not know the reason for this difference between the children. In discussion with some teachers of the deaf in Brazil, in a group that included deaf, deafened, and hearing teachers, they suggested that perhaps some children had learned to count watching a hearing signer whereas others had learned from a deaf signer. They pointed out that those amongst them who were born deaf signed numbers and pointed to the objects at the same time; in contrast one of them, deafened at age 12, counted in sign as hearing people seem to do, pointing with one hand and signing the numbers with the other hand. This difference may be meaningless but may have some effect on deaf children's learning to count. They may find it more congenial to their cognitive style to sign as they point than to organize the activity in a sequential manner. There is, however, no research on this, so far as I know. The point is made here as a stimulus for parents and teachers to develop their own observations of how their deaf children prefer to count in sign, and to find out whether this makes any difference.

Children's creative use of counting to solve sums

It is now very well established that hearing children start school with some knowledge of all four arithmetic operations. This knowledge is informal, as discussed in Chapter 1, and is based on their physical experiences with objects and social experiences, which involve counting and interpersonal situations. A common interpersonal experience of young children is to share, and they seem to learn to share using a 'one-for-you' and 'one-for-me' rule. There is much evidence showing that 4- and 5-year-olds are able to share discontinuous quantities (i.e. quantities where the units are separate and which can be counted) effectively and form equal size quotas (Davis and Hunting, 1990; Davis and Pitkethly, 1990; Davis and Pepper, 1992; Frydman, 1990). With experience, they also realize that if they use the one-for-you and one-for-me procedure the sets they form are of exactly the same size. If they count the number of sweets they have after sharing, for example, and know that they have eight, they know that the other recipient also has eight sweets; they realize they do not need to count the other set.

There are two lines of research on children's informal knowledge of arithmetic: one focuses on children's procedures to solve sums and the other focuses on the difficulty of different types of problems. This chapter considers the research on children's procedures to solve sums, particularly those which are designed by the children without the intervention of teachers. Problem-solving will be analysed later, in Chapters 3 and 4.

A huge amount of interest in how people solve sums was sparked by investigations of long-term memory. It had been assumed for a long time that the way people solve, for example, addition sums is by learning number facts and retrieving these facts from memory. Groen and Parkman (1972) suggested that this belief was 'one of the chief bases for the way arithmetic is taught, a child's ability to add two digits being viewed as evidence that he has memorized an association between the two digits and their sum' (p. 329). Groen and Parkman questioned this assumption and pointed out that there was no empirical support for it. Their analysis was that this assumption is based on the idea that memory for addition works by means of a *reproductive process* – that is, by means of the recording and retrieval of facts. But reproductive theories of memory, they argued, were found to be a faulty explanation and did not fit with the facts known about everyday memory. The deficiencies of this reproductive memory theory led to the development of a theory of *reconstructive memory processes*, which suggests that we remember by generating facts on the basis of rules. The reader will recognize that this argument is the same as that discussed with respect to how we learn to produce thousands of words in a fixed sequence: it was argued that we learn to generate thousands of number labels by knowing, at least implicitly, the rules for generating them.

Groen and Parkman set up an experiment, which they expected would allow for a choice between reproductive or reconstructive memory as an explanation for how children solve one-digit sums. The crucial element in their study was the analysis of how long it took children to solve different addition questions. Their view was that if the reproductive memory theory is correct it should take no longer to add 4 + 5 than 6 + 3, for example, because there is no reason to think that it takes more time to remember one number fact than the other. However, a reconstructive theory would suggest that we don't necessarily remember number facts, but that we find the answer from some sort of internal counting process. If this reconstructive theory is correct, it should take longer to solve 4 + 5 than 6 + 3, because it would take longer to count 5 on from 4 than 3 on from 6. Note that the two sums add up to 9, an important form of control in their experiment. Groen and Parkman presented many one-digit sums to children in their first year of school and analysed the children's reaction time. They measured the reaction time by projecting the sums on a screen, controlled by a computer, and having the children respond by pressing the right answer in the computer keyboard. The computer automatically recorded the time elapsed between the appearance of the question and the child's response. If the children were simply retrieving the answer from memory, there should be no difference between sums such as 4 + 5 and 6 + 3, for example. If the children were using some form of internal counting, it should take longer to find the answer to the first, 4 + 5.

Groen and Parkman thought that different children might use different ways of counting when solving the sums. For example, one child may always count on from the digit that appeared on the left of the screen – thus in 6 + 3 the child would count on from 6 and in 3 + 6 the child would count on from 3. This means that this child would take longer to solve 3 + 6 than to solve 6 + 3. In contrast, another child might realize that 3 + 6 and 6 + 3 actually give the same answer, and count on from 6 irrespective of whether the question was 3 + 6 or 6 + 3. Note that this second, hypothetical child would be showing an understanding of the logical principle of commutativity – that is, this child would know, at least implicitly, that the order of the numbers in the addition question does not affect the result.

Groen and Parkman worked with US children in their first year of school, whose mean age was 6 years and 10 months. Their teacher said that they had been taught the addition facts but they had not been taught to use counting to solve sums. So it would be reasonable to expect that their response times would fit the reproductive memory theory rather than the reconstructive memory theory. The researchers tested this fit individually: for each of the 37 children who took part in the experiment they analysed how long it took the children to answer 55 one-digit addition sums. They found that for the majority of the children (20 of the 37), the reaction times were best described by a reconstructive theory of memory – if the addition sum required them to count up a larger number of units, it took them longer to answer the problem. Interestingly, most children seemed implicitly to use the commutativity principle: it took them as long to answer the question 'What is 3 + 6?' as it did to answer 'What is 6 + 3?'.

Groen and Parkman concluded that children use reconstructive processes in solving one-digit addition sums even when they have been asked to memorize number facts and have been encouraged to try to reproduce them from memory. Thus they identified a creative use of counting by children: though the children were not taught to count to solve sums, they did use counting and in a sophisticated manner – for example, combining the counting procedure with an implicit understanding of commutativity.

Groen and Resnick (1977) later investigated the development of children's addition by teaching even younger children in preschool to solve addition problems through counting. They showed preschoolers, who had not been taught number facts, how to find the answer to single-digit addition sums by putting out the right number of blocks for the first addend, then putting out the right number of blocks for the second addend, and then counting all the blocks together. So they showed the children a strategy that is named 'count all', because the children create a representation for each addend with blocks and then count all the blocks. Groen and Resnick gave the children a large number of practice items on addition over a few days. Opportunity to practise a skill often allows people to develop more efficient ways of getting to the solution. Groen and Resnick observed that, after practice, many children were using a strategy that they had not been taught. Instead of representing each addend with the blocks and then counting all, they were representing only the *smaller* of the two numbers with blocks, and then counting on from the larger. They had been taught one procedure – count all – but had discovered a more efficient procedure – count on from the larger addend. Thus Groen and Resnick showed that, with experience, young children do invent new ways of using counting to solve problems.

This ingenious work analysing how long it takes children to answer addition sums shows that hearing children are very clever in their informal knowledge of mathematics: they can understand the logic of addition so well that they can use the commutativity principle, which they were not taught, to solve problems, given the conditions of practice. What about deaf children?

Two independent studies, one carried out in England and the second in Scotland, showed that deaf children are just as clever. In both studies, the addition sums the children were asked covered a wider range than in the studies by Groen and colleagues, and included all possible combinations of the single digits, with totals reaching up to 18.

In the first study, carried out by Hitch, Arnold and Phillips (1983), the deaf children were attending a special school and were being educated orally. Their mean age was 10 years 2 months. Because of their delay on counting and other mathematical skills, they were matched for mathematics ability to a group of younger hearing children, whose mean age was 6 years 11 months. Hitch and colleagues found that the pattern of responses that fitted the hearing children's response times was the same pattern that fitted the deaf children's response times; both groups had reaction times that fitted with the strategy that Groen and Resnick called 'counting on from the larger number'.

Mulhern and Budge (1993), concerned that this creative use of counting might only appear in deaf children with less severe hearing loss and educated orally, such as those who participated in the study by Hitch et al., decided to replicate this study with prelingually, profoundly deaf children being educated in a total communication system – in this case, Signed English. They worked with youngsters whose mean age was 12 years 4 months, and compared them to a group of hearing children in the same age range, randomly selected from an Edinburgh school in a working-class area. Although Mulhern and Budge did not match the deaf and hearing children on counting and mathematical ability but on age, their analysis of reaction times to addition questions produced the same results observed by Hitch and his colleagues. There was a clear similarity between the response patterns that described the hearing and deaf pupils' behaviour. Thus these two independent studies reached the same conclusion: that deaf pupils, like hearing pupils, can invent creative ways to solve problems through counting and do not have to rely on the reproductive memory of number facts.

It may seem disappointing that the studies that investigated deaf children's creative use of counting to solve problems have been carried out with older children than the hearing children in the original studies. However, the reader should remember that it is necessary to set up a fair comparison in order to understand why deaf children fall behind in mathematics. A fair comparison requires that deaf children should know the counting string in order to use it creatively – and, by now, it has become clear that learning to count takes deaf children longer than it takes hearing children.

The research should be seen in a positive light: once deaf children learn to count, they perform as cleverly as hearing children in tasks where they can use counting to solve problems. But skill improves with experience – and it is necessary to provide deaf children with more experience so that they do not fall behind their hearing peers.

The signed algorithm: deaf children's own invention

In the study by Groen and Resnick, preschool children were taught to represent the numbers in the addition sum with blocks and then count the blocks. However, this is not how young children solve addition problems most often: they tend to use their fingers instead of objects. Preschool hearing children can, for example, lift up 7 fingers and count up from 8 to solve the sum $8 + 7$. Hearing children use their fingers to represent each unit that composes a number – thus they need 7 fingers to represent the 7 units in the number 7 – and they can then count on. What happens if a deaf child who uses BSL wants to solve problems counting on their fingers? They need the fingers to sign the counting numbers, so they cannot use the fingers to represent the units. If they lift up 7 fingers as the units to be counted, how are they going to count in sign? Are deaf signers then restricted to the use of verbal reproductive memory of number facts when learning addition and subtraction?

We (Nunes and Moreno, 1998a) observed in eight different schools many hours of mathematics instruction offered to deaf children both in mainstream schools with units and in special schools. These observations showed that teachers did emphasize the drill of number facts but they also used blocks to teach the children how to solve sums – especially if the children were older and were already working with tens and units. However, we noticed that some children had a method for solving addition and subtraction sums that most teachers were unaware of; only one teacher had noticed it and two children in her class used this method. As far as we know, this method is not taught and had no name. The children who used it believed it was their own way of solving problems – they did not learn it from someone else. We named their method the *signed algorithm*.

The interest of a method that appears to be spontaneously developed by deaf children is obvious: the children might have found a psychologically sensible approach for themselves, which could benefit other children. Apart from the practical significance that the method might have, it also has a theoretical significance. Though there is a vast amount of research on hearing children's own, informal methods, there is almost no research on deaf children's informal methods – and children's own methods tell us about their reasoning. Knowing more about deaf children's own methods would allow researchers to stop asking the question 'Can they do this as well as hearing children?' and start asking 'How do they prefer to do this?'

BSL numbers are signed with one hand. The algorithm involves signing each of the numbers in an addition or subtraction sum with a different hand and operating with the signs. It must be kept in mind that the children are not using the fingers to represent each unit in a number: they are signing the numbers. For example, the number 7 is not represented by 7 fingers, but by the sign for 7 as displayed in Figure 2.1.

When the children wanted to calculate, for example, 8 + 7, they would sign 8 on one hand and 7 on the other hand. The hand on which the numbers are signed would depend on whether the child is right- or left-handed, because one number – the number that they will operate on – is signed on the passive hand (the pad) and the other number is signed on the active hand. In order to solve 8 + 7, 8 is signed, say, on the left, 7 on the right; increments of one are then added to 8 while, at the same time, 7 is decreased by one. In other words, the child counts down from 7 as he/she counts up from 8. When the child reaches 0 on the right hand, the number signed on the left hand indicates the answer. In subtraction, the child needs to count backwards simultaneously with both hands. For example, to solve 16 – 9, the child will sign 16 on the left hand, 9 on the right, and then reduce each number by one – that is, count backwards – until the right hand reaches 0. The answer will be read from the left hand.

The use of the signed algorithm is quite different from the use of fingers by hearing children. When hearing children use their fingers to solve a sum, their fingers represent the units to be counted and any three fingers, for example, can represent the number 3. The fingers can be counted in any order because they are representing each unit, and thus the order in which the fingers are added or taken away does not matter. This is termed an analogue representation of numbers (Brissiaud, 1992). In contrast, when deaf children use the signed algorithm, 3 can be signed only in the conventional manner, with the index, middle and ring fingers extended and the hand help upwards. Three other extended fingers – the thumb, index and middle fingers – with the hand held horizontally is the sign for 8. Yet three other extended fingers – the middle, index and small fingers – do not represent anything in the system described in Figure 2.1. So if the deaf child were to treat the fingers as units and perform the operations by indiscriminately extending and retracting fingers, the result might be a completely different number or even a non-number. BSL numbers are referred to as a conventional, symbolic representation of numbers.

The use of the signed algorithm offers BSL users an option that does not require them to remember verbal number facts: they can produce the answer to any number fact using their own counting system.

The information that we have so far on the consequences of teaching the signed algorithm systematically is quite limited. We observed one teacher in a London primary school for the deaf and her six pupils, who were all profoundly deaf and were being educated through Sign Supported English. None of the children had a disability apart from hearing loss and only one had deaf parents. The children's age range was 6 to 8 years, with a mean of 7 years 4 months; they were attending Year 2. The aim of the study was to analyse what difficulties the children encountered in learning the signed algorithm when it is formally taught and to see how the children used this algorithm to solve addition and subtraction story problems. So the children were video-taped during six mathematics lessons and compared in their problem-solving ability with a group of same-aged deaf children in another special school where they were not exposed to the signed algorithm.

In all the six lessons, the teacher's main aim was to teach the signed algorithm. She made the activities fun for the children but the sums were not used to solve story problems, with the exception of the first lesson, where the children practised addition to calculate the total cost of two items in a pretend shop. A brief description of the lessons is offered here.

Lesson 1

A number of objects, such as balloons, baubles and tinsel (the lessons took place before Christmas) were placed on a table, tagged and priced with numbers under 10. Each child was given a purse filled with penny coins. Each child chose two objects and, using the signed algorithm, added the values of the two objects. The teacher then asked the child to provide the correct amount of money to 'pay' for the objects. Each child had several turns to buy items. All the children watched while one performed the purchases. After the group session, each child worked individually (with the assistance of an adult). A worksheet compiled by the teacher was handed out. The worksheet had drawings of the objects used in the group session, all priced. The children were required to solve a series of written questions such as: lolly + tinsel = ?. The child was required to add, again using the signed algorithm, and to write the answer on the sheet.

Lesson 2

Sheets of A4 paper (21) numbered from 0 to 20 were placed in numerical order on the floor, as if this were a huge board game. One child stood on the first piece of paper, numbered 0. The other children pulled a card from a file with a number on it, one at a time, and read the number. Using the signed algorithm, the child who was in the game had to add the number to his/her current position and then move to the indicated result. Each child had a turn in the game. The game was played again with the children starting on number 20 and subtracting the values, moving backwards.

Lesson 3

This lesson was dedicated to practice in counting backwards, a necessary skill for good performance in the signed algorithm. The children had several turns at counting backwards from a number written on a card they had taken from a pile. Then they practised subtraction sums.

Lesson 4

This lesson was dedicated to practising subtraction. The sums were written on cards, which the children drew out from a pile on the table. The teacher started the session by placing blocks on the table and asking what would happen if some blocks were added and what would happen if some blocks were taken away. She then compared taking blocks away with counting backwards using sign; the children counted backwards as the blocks were taken away from the table. All values were up to 10. The teacher also instructed the children to stretch out their arms as they signed 10 and to draw their arms closer to themselves as they counted down.

This practice of counting down was followed by colouring a Father Christmas drawing done as a puzzle. Each piece contained a sum in it.

The children had to carry out the sum and use the result to find out from a chart what colour corresponded to that number. The number could be the result of different addition or subtraction sums: for example, the number 3 corresponded to red and it could be the result of 5 – 2 or 7 – 4 or 2 + 1 etc.

Lesson 5

This lesson took the form of a bingo game. Each child was given a card with numbers. The teacher presented operations to be solved. The children had to establish the answer to the operation and then check their cards.

Lesson 6

The children worked in pairs during this lesson in order to play a board game, where their counters were placed at the head of a snake and moved towards the tail. The moves were determined by the result of sums that were written on cards, which they drew from a pile of cards. The children were only allowed to make the move if their calculation was correct.

The observations made it clear that the children enjoyed the lessons and became much more able in providing the answers for the sums. However, it should be noted that the lessons' aims were drill and practice of the signed algorithm, not problem-solving. In this sense, the lessons fit with the teaching referred to as 'traditional', where the emphasis is on drill and not reasoning.

After the teacher had completed the lessons she had planned with this aim, one experimenter saw the children individually and asked each one to solve a sample of sums with values up to 20. The sums were presented on separate cards. These sessions were also tape-recorded to provide a description of the difficulties of the signed algorithm.

Past research with hearing children learning the written algorithms for multidigit addition and subtraction has shown that children tend to make systematic mistakes during the learning process. These mistakes – called *bugs* by analogy to errors in computer programs, which generate systematic faults in the output – have been widely described in the literature (see, for example, Brown and VanLehn, 1982; Resnick, 1982; Young and O'Shea, 1981). Two examples are the bugs *failure to carry* and *taking the smaller from the bigger*. *Failure to carry* appears in an addition sum when two units added produce a number higher than 10; for example, in the sum 18 + 26, the child would add 8 and 6, write 4 in the units place and forget to add the ten to the other tens, obtaining the answer 34.

Taking the smaller from the bigger is an error that appears in subtraction; for example, in the sum 23 – 15, the child attempts to subtract 5 from 3 in the units place, thinks that this is impossible, so the child subtracts 3 from 5, writes down 2, and then completes the subtraction, ending with 12 as the result. The descriptions of bugs in written algorithms show that the bugs are directly related to the steps the children are taught and to the nature of the numbers they are manipulating. Failure to carry happens because the child is adding the numbers in the units place, using written numbers – the mistake would not appear if the child were, for example, counting 6 on from 18, and thus using oral numbers to find the answer. Similarly, subtracting the smaller from the bigger is a result of operating with the units place of a written number separately from the rest of the number: if the child were counting back from 23, say, the child would not even consider the question 3 – 5.

These mistakes show that the description of algorithms should consider whether they produce systematic errors and how difficult it is for children to overcome these errors. The bugs in written algorithms have proven much harder to eliminate than teachers expected them to be. Thus our investigation (Nunes and Moreno, 1998b) of the signed algorithm was aimed at describing possible bugs and their consequences for the learning process, as well as the use of the algorithm to solve problems later.

The analysis of the video-tapes showed that children have to conquer a number of difficulties before the signed algorithm is mastered. The children's error types were classified into three different categories.

First, the children must ensure that they do not confuse fingers as countable objects with fingers used in signing the numbers. In the first lessons, some children did not seem to realize the completely conventional nature of the computation process and added or subtracted fingers without concern for making sure that they were counted up or down. This led to wrong answers as well as non-answers, when the fingers that remained did not represent a signed number. These mistakes were only observed early on in the learning process and had been eliminated by the time the children were assessed after the six lessons.

Second, the children need to become experts in counting down in signed numbers. This skill, which hearing children use only in subtraction, is necessary in both addition and subtraction with the signed algorithm. Two types of errors were observed while the children were still unskilled in counting down. One mistake we named *skipping 5*. When the children are counting down from a number larger than 5, they need to retract the thumb with the hand in the horizontal position (going from 6 to 5) and then retract the thumb again with the hand in the vertical position (going from 5 to 4). Some children retracted the thumb once only

– when they were counting down from 6 – and went directly to 4. Interestingly, as they became experts in counting down they seemed to hold on to the thumb while they twisted the hand from the horizontal to the vertical position and then retract the thumb. Though difficult to describe, the gesture was rather elegant, and treated the change in position as the element that marks the counting down. The other mistake we named *failure to carry*, owing to its similarity to the bug described earlier on in the written algorithm. BSL changes rules for generating numbers at 5 and 10. When the children displayed a failure to carry the 5 error, they were, for example, counting down from 8; they retracted the fingers in the correct order and reached a closed hand, after retracting the thumb in counting down from 6 to 5. Instead of moving on to 5, they stopped, as if they had reached 0. So if they were adding, for example, 8 on to 7, they would end up with 10 as the answer.

A third error type appears to result from the need to coordinate two counting actions. As described earlier, one number is operated on, signed with the passive hand, whereas the other is added to or subtracted from it. Occasionally the children appeared to forget which number was which, reversed the role of the hands, and started to implement the transformation with the passive hand. For example, subtracting 6 from 9, the child is counting down from 6 and from 9 at the same time; after implementing the process on two units, arriving at 4 on the active hand and 7 on the passive hand, the child then tries to subtract 7 from 4. This confusion between the active and passive hands changes the problem into its reverse: 7 – 4 becomes 4 – 7. If the child continues to count down on both hands, the child arrives at 0 – 3 and does not know what to do next. Some children give 0 as the answer, some children start again. This error was observed only occasionally in two children at the testing session after the lessons.

During the teaching sessions, it was observed that the teacher provided the children with a model for solving the sums that assumed they understood the commutativity of addition: independently of the order of the numbers on the cards she used to present the sums, she always signed the larger number with the passive hand, thus using the strategy of counting on from the larger. Thus regardless of whether she presented a card showing 5 + 9 or 9 + 5, she counted on from 9, signing 9 with the passive hand. This did cause some confusion during the acquisition process, though not for all the children. In the testing session, only the most skilful child systematically used the method of counting on from the larger in all the sums. The remaining five children used it sometimes and sometimes calculated in the order that the numbers appeared on paper. The training sessions had not been sufficient for them to develop the more economical strategy of counting on from the larger number.

The observation of the teaching process and the difficulties posed by the signed algorithm showed that the difficulties were mostly temporary. After six teaching sessions, the children had reached a very good level of mastery of the algorithm. So the children now had acquired the ability to use a system and control their computation processes, and were no longer left to the less controllable process of trying to recall a verbal number fact.

This study did not include a comparison with hearing children of the children who learned the signed algorithm. They were, though, compared with eight deaf children in the same age range, attending Year 2 in another special school for the deaf; the comparison children were not being taught the signed algorithm. Unfortunately, this comparison did not include simple sums but only considered the children's success in solving arithmetic story problems. The children were asked to solve ten addition and subtraction story problems, four of which were of the simplest type whereas the other six involved other difficulties beyond that of computation. Only the results of the four simple problems are considered here: the difficulties of different types of problems will be considered in Chapter 3, and the signed algorithm will be discussed again in that context. The children who had been taught the signed algorithm solved 3.6 problems correctly; the children who had not been taught the algorithm solved 2.4 problems correctly. This difference was statistically significant even though the number of children in the study was so small. Thus the signed algorithm can be taught and used to solve arithmetic problems.

The significance of the algorithm stems from the fact that it was developed by the children themselves. This means that is must be appropriate for deaf children. The study of its transmission by a teacher shows that it can be taught and that the initial difficulties can be surmounted as the children become more skilled. It would be too hasty to conclude that it should be taught in all schools to all children who sign. There is simply not sufficient research to support such a wide-ranging claim. However, the evidence suggests that it could be useful for deaf children to have at their disposal a method that they can control better than verbal recall. It is clear that further research is urgently needed about deaf children's own methods of solving sums and that the signed algorithm is an example of deaf children's creative use of their own counting system.

Conclusion

This chapter examined the question: 'When do deaf children start to show difficulties with mathematics?'

It is known that hearing children have much informal knowledge of mathematics prior to starting school: they can mentally represent numbers in order to copy arrays using the same number of objects and they start to learn to count and use the their knowledge of counting creatively, to solve addition and subtraction problems. Psychologists have argued that this informal knowledge is the basis for successfully learning mathematics in school. Thus it is important to check whether deaf children develop informal mathematical knowledge.

Research has shown that deaf preschoolers are as competent at some of the informal mathematical knowledge tasks as their hearing peers. Deaf 3- and 4-year-olds can represent and reproduce the right number of objects in arrays whether the arrays are presented spatially or sequentially. They are actually better than the hearing children if the arrays are presented spatially. This suggests that deaf children have some information processing strengths which could be used in designing instruction especially suited to their preferences in information processing.

However, there is much research that shows that deaf people find recalling items in a particular sequence – serial recall – more difficult than hearing people do. This means that it is more difficult for deaf children to learn to count, because counting requires serial recall of the number words. In order to count correctly, it is necessary to remember the number words in their exact order every time. It has been documented that deaf children do find it more difficult to learn to count, whether in English or BSL. Once they master the counting string, they are as good as hearing children in showing flexibility in its use. These observations suggest that teachers of deaf preschoolers should give them more opportunities to practise counting than they would normally offer to hearing children. It is possible that deaf children start to fall behind simply through lack of experience with counting.

Another consideration raised in the studies reviewed here was that memory – and particularly memory for the counting string – is not simply a matter of recording and retrieving words in a fixed order. Counting systems are not learned through simple reproductive memory but through reconstructive memory, which uses rules to reconstruct the number words in sequence. Some researchers raised the possibility that rule-learning might be a process that depends on oral language – and thus would be more difficult for deaf children. However, research with children aged between 3 and 6 years showed that deaf children perform as well as hearing children in rule-learning tasks – and actually performed better when the rule to be learned was tactile.

Research has also shown that hearing children develop informal methods for solving arithmetic sums which they have not been taught. Some researchers raised the hypothesis that perhaps this creative use of counting to solve sums would be a privilege of hearing people, possibly extended to deaf people educated orally. However, evidence from work with prelingually, profoundly deaf pupils shows that they too use counting creatively to solve sums.

Finally, it was considered that so far the research on deaf children concentrated too much on what hearing children do and whether deaf children can do the same. Little work is available on deaf children's own inventions in informal mathematics. The description of the signed algorithm is a notable exception. The signed algorithm is a method designed by deaf children educated in BSL to solve sums using signed numbers. Within the confines of the little research available, it is possible to conclude that it could be taught to deaf children with positive results. However, it is necessary to be cautious before introducing new procedures into the mathematics curriculum for the deaf, so it is concluded that more research is urgently needed on deaf children's own informal mathematical knowledge, and their characteristics, advantages and difficulties.

CHAPTER 3

Additive reasoning: connecting addition and subtraction

Psychologists and educators have discussed for more than half a century a number of questions related to how children learn about addition and subtraction. Despite much progress in our knowledge in this domain, it would be too much to claim that this chapter offers a synthesis of these ideas. There is still much dispute about the facts and disagreements about the theories. So what aims can this chapter have?

The chapter will, from the start, take one side in this dispute. One theoretical view is that, in order to solve arithmetic story problems, children must understand the problem, represent it with numbers, choose the correct operation and then carry out the calculation. It was argued in Chapter 1 that there is sufficient evidence to show that this theoretical approach is not supported by research. Children do need to construct an appropriate mental representation of the problem, and carry out manipulations that relate to this representation, but the representation could take different forms and so could the path to solution. Computation procedures – such as an addition or a subtraction operation – do not represent the essence of mathematical concepts. In order to have a theory of the development of mathematical concepts that is useful for teaching, we need to find a theory that represents the mathematical concepts appropriately.

Following Vergnaud's theory, it was proposed that, when considering a mathematical concept, it is necessary to analyse the *logic* of the concept, the *systems of signs* used to represent it, and the *situations* in which the concept is used. Consistent with this theory, in this chapter it will be argued that the operations of addition and subtraction are *procedures* related to the same core logical principles – and therefore they should be analysed and taught as different aspects of the *same* concept. Vergnaud refers to the overarching concept that includes both of these procedures as 'additive reasoning' or 'additive structures'.

What is at the core of additive reasoning?

There is – surprisingly – much agreement in this respect: *the core of additive reasoning is defined by part–whole relations*. All the different problem types related to additive reasoning are based on the logic of part–whole relations.

The part–whole logic can be used to solve different arithmetic problems. You can have two parts (or more, of course) and put them together to form a whole: this would give a simple example of what has traditionally been called an *addition problem*. You can have a whole and take a part away from it: this is a prototypical example of a *subtraction problem*. But it should be noted that these definitions are based on the procedure used to solve the problem, not on the logic that guides the procedures. This chapter will show that a conception based on procedures is not helpful in defining the operations of thought that children need to carry out in order to solve different types of problems. This conception is therefore not helpful in explaining why two problems that can be solved by means of the same operation can have radically different levels of difficulty.

It is possible to create a large number of story problems that fit this part–whole logic. Story problems can differ in *content*: for example, one problem might be about a girl eating some sweets and asking how many sweets were left; another story problem might be about a boy who played marbles then lost some, and asking how many marbles had he left at the end of the game. Research has shown that differences in the content of the problems are not related to children's success in problem-solving, so long as there are no other differences between the problems.

So, what does make one problem more difficult than another? This chapter is organized in three sections, which analyse three types of situations where the logic of part–whole is relevant. Within each section, variations in problem structure that affect problem difficulty are considered, as well as the different systems of signs that children can use when solving numerical problems. Some of the issues discussed are those that render problems difficult for all children, hearing and deaf; but deaf children's specific difficulties as well as ways of attempting to address them will also be considered. The chapter does not attempt to cover all the issues related to additive reasoning but only to illustrate the most significant ones. For comprehensive reviews, the reader is referred to other sources (Carpenter and Moser, 1982; Nunes and Bryant, 1996; Riley, Greeno and Heller, 1983; Vergnaud, 1982; Vershaffel and De Corte, 1997).

Situation type 1: change problems

What defines a change problem is that, in the story it tells, there is an initial quantity, then an event or action changes this quantity, then there is an end-result of the change. The number of possible events and actions that change quantities is very large: think of what happens when you have some sweets and you receive sweets as a present; you eat some sweets; you give some sweets away; you lose some sweets; some sweets get too old and you throw them away; your brother pinches some of your sweets and so on. The number of sweets changes; in some cases you end up with less, in other cases you end up with more.

Most often, when children are asked to solve arithmetic problems that involve change in the quantities, they are asked to produce a numerical answer. The English psychologist Martin Hughes (1986) asked preschool hearing children, in the age range 3 to 5 years, to solve some arithmetic problems in his Box Task. Here is how the Box Task worked.

Martin Hughes (MH) put two bricks in the box and shut the lid. He then asked Gordon (G), aged 4 years 8 months and attending the nursery in the Psychology Department in Edinburgh, how many bricks were in the box.

G: Two.
MH: (Adds one brick in such a way that Gordon sees it going in but cannot see into the box.) How many now?
G: Three.
MH: I'm putting one more in. (Adds one more, the same way.)
G: Four. Four!
MH: And now I'm putting in two more. (Does so.)
G: Six! Six!
MH: (Takes one brick out.) How many now?
G: (Pause.) Five. Five!
MH: (Takes two out but does not have to ask the question.)
G: Three! (Hughes, 1986: 25–6.)

Hughes' work both illustrates young children's informal mathematical knowledge well, and clearly documents their ability both to understand transformations that increase and decrease quantities, and to provide a numerical answer to problems with either type of transformation. Yet, as they are in nursery school, they still have not been taught arithmetic: they do not know the procedures for computing addition and subtraction sums.

Hughes observed that the young children in his study answered 83% of the Box Task questions correctly. They were also good at answering problems about a hypothetical box, in which case, Hughes did not have a box in front of them – he just asked them to imagine that he was putting blocks in or taking blocks out of the box. Their success rate was 56% in

this imaginary Box Task. In contrast, when he asked them to solve sums –
e.g. 'Tell me, what is three and one more?' – their success rate decreased
considerably: it was only 15%. Hughes showed that young children can
solve transformation problems with small numbers quite well but that
they do not know 'the correct operation'. His findings are in perfect
agreement with the idea that addition and subtraction computation are
just one procedure, but not the only route to problem-solving.

With respect to young hearing children's ability to understand transformations, his results do not leave room for doubt: preschool hearing
children understand transformations and do so well enough to provide
numerical answers.

There is little work on young deaf children's problem-solving ability,
though there is some research with children at the beginning of primary
school. The question we need to consider is whether it could be more difficult for deaf than for hearing children to solve transformation problems.
From the research reviewed in the preceding chapter, we know that deaf
children have difficulty with serial recall when the task places higher levels of demand on their memory, though they perform well if the task does
not impose a high level of memory demand. A transformation problem
contains at least three pieces of information; for example, in the Box Task,
the child needs to remember how many bricks were in the box, that the
transformation was to put more bricks in, and the number of bricks that
were put in. Does this place such high demands on deaf preschoolers'
memory that they will have difficulty in solving the problem?

Unfortunately there is no research to answer this question so far. But
there is one study that provides relevant information, although the task is
different. Moreno (2000) told hearing and deaf children a story problem
about a transformation that either increased or decreased the initial quantity in the story. She presented the children with two pictures (see Figure
3.1 for an example) and asked them to indicate which picture showed the
beginning and which showed the end of the story. For example, one story
was: 'A boy had some toys. Then Daddy gave him some toys.' The children
were shown two pictures, one of a boy with 2 toys and the other of the
same boy with 6 toys. The children were asked to repeat the story and
then indicate which of the two pictures showed the boy in the beginning
of the story and which one showed the boy at the end of the story. Moreno
reasoned that, if the children understood the consequence of the transformation – Daddy gave him some toys – they would indicate the picture
where the boy had 2 toys as showing the beginning of the story and the
picture with 6 toys as showing the end of the story. Because the transformation increased the number of toys the boy had, the picture where he
had fewer toys should correspond to the beginning and the one with
more toys should correspond to the end of the story.

Making inferences from change

The boy had some toys.
Then Daddy gave him some toys.
(The child repeats the story.)
One picture shows what happened first and
  the other shows the end of the story.
Which picture shows the beginning of the
  story?

Figure 3.1 An item from Moreno's Change Task (reproduced from Moreno, 2000, with permission).

Moreno reasoned that by asking the children to make an inference that connected the story with the pictures, she was increasing the task demands in the same way that arithmetic problems do; for example, in order to count up or count down in the Box Task developed by Hughes, the children had to make an inference about how the quantities were changing – were they increasing or decreasing? Moreno used a task where the children did not have to give a numerical answer, because she knew that earlier studies had shown that hearing children have a better knowledge of the counting string. Thus if the deaf children had more difficulty than the hearing children in this non-quantitative task, this would indicate that the demands of remembering events in sequence and making inferences about how the states before and after the event are connected, are difficult for deaf children.

The deaf and hearing children in her study were matched for age, and had a mean age of 8 years 2 months. The level of hearing loss varied: 14 children had mild to severe loss and 18 had severe or profound loss. They were educated in different language environments, and Moreno used with them the form of communication used in their school. All the children were attending state-supported schools in London. The hearing children attended one of the mainstream schools with a unit for deaf children; some of the deaf children attended the same school, whereas others attended other mainstream schools with units, or special schools for the deaf.

The children answered eight questions in the Change Task. The task was quite easy for the hearing children: their mean number of correct responses was 6.7. In contrast, this task proved rather difficult for the deaf children: their mean number of correct responses was 3. This difference was statistically significant.

Thus the deaf children found it difficult to cope with the demands of a serial recall task where they had to simultaneously make inferences about how the events changed the quantity in the problem. This difficulty could not be attributed to a limited knowledge of the counting string, because the task did not require a numerical answer. This suggests that it is necessary to design instruction procedures for deaf children that will support them in keeping in mind the information in the order of the events and simultaneously making inferences about how quantities are changed.

Different types of change problems require different operations of thought

A change problem is defined, as indicated earlier on, by an initial quantity, a change in the quantity, and a final state. So it is possible to create problems that have different structures: (1) we can tell a story that says what the initial quantity was, what the value of the change was, and then ask what the end result was; (2) we can tell a story that says what the initial and the final quantities were, and then ask what the value of the change was; (3) we can tell a story that says what the value of the change was, what the end result was, and then ask what the initial quantity was. These problem structures are conventionally represented by using 'x' to indicate the quantity that the child has to calculate and the letters 'a' and 'b' to indicate the quantities that were mentioned in the story. Table 3.1 presents an overview of the problem types with an example of each.

The situations in all the problems are change situations. If the problems were solved by means of an arithmetic operation, two sums ($5 + 3$ or $8 - 3$) would be sufficient to lead directly from the questions to the solution. Yet the level of difficulty of these problems is radically different because the different problem structures mean that different operations of thought are required. The order in level of difficulty is the same for both hearing and deaf children (Frostad and Ahlberg, 1999; Hyde, Zevenbergen and Power, 2003; Nunes and Moreno, 1998a).

Two of these problems are the easiest and are of comparable level of difficulty: $a + b = x$ and $a - b = x$. Although the first is related to an addition procedure and the second to a subtraction procedure, most research indicates that 5- and 6-year-old hearing children have an equally high rate of success in these problems. These problems are often referred to as *direct problems* since the children can achieve the solution by performing a

Table 3.1 Different problem structures in the change situations

---

Change increase

$a + b = x$	A girl had 5 sweets; her granny gave her 3 sweets; how many sweets does she have now?
$a + x = b$	A girl had 3 sweets; her granny gave her some sweets; now she has 8 sweets; how many sweets did her granny give her?
$x + a = b$	A girl had some sweets; her granny gave her 3 sweets; now she has 8 sweets; how many sweets did she have before her granny came to visit?

Change decrease

$a - b = x$	A boy had 8 marbles; he played a game and lost 3 marbles; how many marbles does he have now?
$a - x = b$	A boy had 8 marbles; he played a game and lost some marbles; now he has 3 marbles; how many marbles did he lose in the game?
$x - a = b$	A boy had some marbles; he played a game and lost 3 marbles; now he has 5 marbles; how many marbles did he have before the game?

---

change in the number symbols that is the same change that happened in the story. If the quantity increased, the children can count up or add; if the quantity decreased, the children can count down or subtract.

A comparison between direct problems and those that are called inverse, described as $x + a = b$ and $x - a = b$, is helpful to illustrate what is meant by operations of thought. In an inverse problem where the quantity decreases, the child has to increase the final state by the value of the transformation in order to figure out what the initial quantity was. In psychological terminology, we say that the child has to apply the inverse operation: if the quantity decreased, the child has to either count up or add to find the answer. Thus inverse problems, though they present children with the same amount of information to be recalled as direct problems, are difficult because they demand more operations of thought in the solution process. In information processing terms, inverse problems increase the problem demands because of the inferences that the children have to make while remembering the information.

This analysis indicates that inverse problems should be more difficult than direct problems for all children, deaf and hearing. But it also leads to the hypothesis that deaf and hearing children might not differ in direct problems whereas the deaf children might find the inverse problems significantly more difficult than the hearing children. The increased processing demands in a serial recall task could prove to be a serious obstacle for the deaf children.

Moreno (2000) created a non-computational task where she examined hearing and deaf children's ability to remember a story with a change sequence. Some of the items were similar to direct problems whereas others were similar to inverse problems. In the items analogous to the direct problems, all the elements were mentioned in a sequence. In the items analogous to inverse problems, one item was mentioned but not specified, so the child had to keep in mind a gap where that item fitted in the sequence. One example of each type of item is presented in Figures 3.2a and 3.2b.

(a)

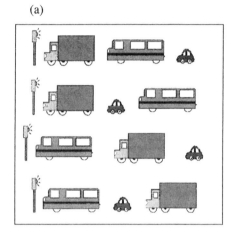

All items are mentioned in sequence

There was a bus waiting at the traffic lights; next arrived a lorry; next arrived a car.

(b)

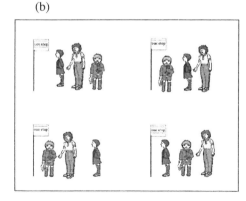

Operation required: to keep a gap in the sequence

There were some people waiting at the bus stop.
The first person, I don't know who it was.
Next a girl came to wait for the bus.
Next came a lady.

Figure 3.2 (a) Example of a non-computational, direct change problem (reproduced from Moreno, 2000, with permission). (b) Example of a non-computational change problem analogous to inverse problems (reproduced from Moreno, 2000, with permission).

As in her previous task, the children were told the story and then asked to repeat it, and point to a picture that corresponded to the story. Also, as in the previous task, the children's means of communication in school was used in the experiment. This method ensures that the children can reproduce the story, and thus helps eliminate explanations that attribute the children's difficulty with the task to their linguistic difficulties.

Moreno's direct and inverse change problems were non-computational because she wanted to avoid the influence that the deaf children's more restricted knowledge of the counting string might have on their performance in a change problem. Considering that deaf children's difficulties with serial recall are only observed when task demands are high, she expected that they would perform as well as the hearing children in the direct items, where task demands are not high. This would show that they understood the task and could remember the number of items required for correct responses. However, the inverse non-computation tasks increase task demands without increasing the number of items to be recalled. If the deaf children find non-computational, inverse problems more challenging than hearing children do, their difficulty cannot be explained by differences in their knowledge of counting. It must reflect differences in information processing. This result would clarify why deaf children fall behind in arithmetic problem-solving and could give some indication of what type of resources might benefit deaf children's learning.

The children who solved this task were the same 42 deaf and 37 of the 69 hearing children who answered the Change Task.

As predicted by Moreno, there was no difference between the deaf and the hearing children in the direct, non-computational items. Both groups performed very well on the task and had a mean number of correct responses above 7 in the eight items that they had been asked to solve. The inverse items were significantly more difficult for both groups of children, showing that having to keep in mind a gap in a sequence of events does increase task demands. The hearing children performed significantly better than the deaf children in the inverse, non-computational task: the mean number correct in the eight items was 6 for the hearing children and 4.5 for the deaf children. This difference was statistically significant.

These results have considerable implications for the design of instruction for deaf children. It is well documented that they have greater difficulty with sequential presentation and serial recall. Change problems are about sequences of events and require serial recall. However, it is quite possible that, if deaf children learn to use their preferred and superior spatial coding ability to represent sequential information, they could improve their problem-solving skill.

Up to now, researchers have suggested that deaf children's difficulties with word problem-solving are explained by their reading difficulties

(Serrano Pau, 1995) or by their difficulty with language comprehension (Barham and Bishop, 1991; Hyde, Zevenbergen and Power, 2003; Serrano Pau, 1995). The educational implication of attributing deaf children's mathematical difficulties to their linguistic difficulties is that more and more time will be devoted to language and literacy teaching, and consequently less time to the teaching of mathematics. Moreno's results suggest that it is important to focus more, not less, on the structure of mathematics problems when teaching deaf children.

A similar point was made by Frostad and Ahlberg (1999), who studied arithmetic story problem-solving by deaf children in Norway. Like Moreno, they ensured that, when communicating with the children, they used the children's own communication system so that there was no doubt about their understanding of the story. Their findings – which will be presented in greater detail a bit later in this chapter – led them to comment that teaching approaches to help deaf children solve story problems must do more than focus on the language used in the problem: 'Children should be given the opportunity to develop their understanding of problem structures and strategies to deal with problems in contexts where inferior text comprehension does not represent a constraint to their problem-solving. On a conceptually based understanding of problem structure, linguistic competence can then be developed' (Frostad and Ahlberg, 1999: 291).

Moreno's results with non-computational problems, considered alongside deaf children's more restricted knowledge of the counting string, lead to the expectation that deaf children can solve direct problems as well as hearing children, if they are matched for knowledge of the counting string. However, they are expected to perform significantly worse in inverse problems for a longer period of time.

Although there are no studies where deaf and hearing children were matched for knowledge of the counting string, comparisons between primary school hearing and deaf children's performance in arithmetic problem-solving confirm these expectations to some extent. Deaf children seem to be about two to two and a half years behind hearing children in their knowledge of the counting string at the beginning of primary school. So by the time they reach their third year in primary school, they should be performing quite similarly to hearing children in direct problems, whereas the gap between the two groups might still persist in inverse problems. Nunes and Moreno (1998a) found that the deaf children in their study, who were in Years 2 to 5 in primary school (age level 8 to 11 years), performed similarly to hearing children in direct change problems but showed a significant delay in inverse problems. Hyde, Zevenbergen and Power (2003), working with deaf pupils in Australia in their first to seventh year in primary school, also obtained similar results. Year 3 deaf pupils performed as well as hearing pupils in problems of the type a + b = x, where the deaf pupils showed 86% correct responses and the hearing pupils showed 90%. The same was observed for problems of the type a – b = x: deaf pupils gave 86% correct responses and hearing pupils 90%. In contrast, in inverse problems there were still significant differences between the deaf and hearing pupils in Year 3: for problems of the type x + a = b, the rate of correct responses was 29% for the deaf and 66% for the hearing pupils, and for problems of the type x – a = b, these percentages were 43% and 65%, respectively.

One novelty of the analysis presented here is that it does not make a uniform prediction that deaf children are behind hearing children in arithmetic word problems: the prediction is of a pattern of specific strengths and difficulties, based on well-documented differences in information processing between the two groups of children. The prediction is supported in both non-computational and computational problems. Further research, where hearing and deaf children are matched for knowledge of the counting string and then compared in word problem-solving, could provide further evidence for the existence of a specific pattern of difficulties for deaf children predicted from their information processing skills. A second novelty from this analysis is that it suggests ways to help deaf children improve their problem-solving skill. These will be discussed in the sections that follow.

Representing information in change problems

There are two types of information to be represented in change problems: the story itself – the series of events – and the numerical information. Research shows that the way children represent both types of information has an impact on their problem-solving ability. Here, number representation is discussed first, followed by the representation of the sequence of events.

Representation of the numerical information

Nunes and Moreno (1997, 1998a) analysed how different ways of representing the *numerical information* influence deaf children's performance. In one study (Nunes and Moreno, 1998a) we gave the same children two problem-solving sessions. In the first session they were offered cut-out drawings of objects to represent the problem information. For example, if the problem mentioned 'a girl' and 'flowers', we set out on the table cut-out drawings of a girl and several flowers. In the second session we offered the children blocks, irrespective of what was mentioned in the problem. Our hypothesis was that, although blocks are manipulatives and can be moved about in the same way as the cut-out objects, they offer the children a weaker support when the children are trying to imagine the situation presented linguistically. The children were the same ones whose problem-solving performance was referred to earlier on in this chapter. In all year groups of primary school (from Year 2 to Year 5), the problem-solving performance was better when the children had cut-out objects than when they had blocks, even though the blocks were regularly used in the classroom when they were representing numbers to calculate sums. Although the difference was small – of 19 problems presented, they solved an average of 10.3 problems correctly with cut-out objects and 8.8 with blocks – the difference was statistically significant and was observed at all age levels.

The children in the second study (Nunes and Moreno, 1996) were the six children who had learned to use the signed algorithm mentioned in the previous chapter. They were asked to solve 16 story problems that could be solved by using sums they had previously solved when asked to demonstrate the signed algorithm. The 16 problems included the different types of additive reasoning situations discussed in this chapter (change, combine and comparison, with the different types of structure that can be created for each situation). In the first problem-solving session, they were asked to solve the story problems using the signed algorithm. In the second session they were offered cut-out objects to represent the numerical information. The mean number of correct responses to the problems was 9.45 (SD = 1.4) when the children had the cut-out objects and 1.98 (SD = 2.2) when they had to use the signed algorithm. This difference was statistically significant. So although the children in this study had no difficulty with the sums, they performed better when they had the cut-out objects to represent the problems than when they answered the questions using signed numbers and applying the algorithm.

Why should the representation of numerical information with cut-out objects produce different results from symbolic numerical representations?

There are two reasons for this. One is the facility with which children imagine a situation when they are offered different types of props. One of the reasons that drawings are extensively used in children's literature is that they increase the children's enjoyment and make it easier for them to imagine the situation in the story. If this also applies to solving arithmetic story problems, the greater enjoyment might be connected to higher levels of motivation, which in turn lead to better performance. The second reason is related to what the representations afford. Manipulative materials can be counted – and thus children can implement informal solutions based on counting, as well as formal solutions connected to sums. However, the representation of eight objects with the number 8 does not allow the children to implement their informal practical strategies (see Nunes, 1997), whereas they can, for example, physically remove 3 from 8 blocks to know the result of '8 take away 3'.

The impact of different ways of representing problems on deaf children's performance was observed also by Frostad and Ahlberg (1999). They did not offer the children different means to represent the number; rather, they observed how the children represented the information and how this, in turn, influenced their solution. They asked 32 deaf children to answer additive reasoning problems with all three types of structure: direct problems (a + b = x or a − b = x), inverse problems (x + a = b or x − a = b), and change-unknown problems (a + x = b or a − x = b). Change-unknown problems differ from both direct and inverse problems in level of difficulty: they are harder than direct but easier than inverse problems. What makes change-unknown problems easier than inverse problems is that children can successfully use informal strategies that match the type of change in the story, increasing or decreasing quantities. For example, the problem 'A girl had 5 sweets; her granny gave her some sweets; now she has 8 sweets; how many sweets did her granny give her?' is an example of a change-unknown problem. Hearing children who implement informal counting strategies will, for example, extend 5 fingers to represent the 5 sweets that the girl had initially. They will then count up to 8, keeping track of how many fingers they had to extend to reach 8. This will tell them that Granny gave the girl 3 sweets. So they use the same type of change described in the problem – they increase 5 until they get to 8 – and do not have to use an inverse operation. It should be pointed out that the arithmetic sum that would be prescribed by school to solve this problem is 8 − 5, which is in no way analogous to what happened in the story.

Frostad and Ahlberg provided detailed descriptions of the deaf children's attempts to solve change-unknown and inverse problems. Some of the children in their examples used signed numbers whereas the others used their fingers to represent the objects, not to represent the number. Here two children's solutions to change-unknown problems will be used to illustrate the point. The example is rephrased to make it intelligible in the absence of the context in which it is described in the original paper. Square brackets are used to indicate that an explanation has been added.

Pia, a 9-year-old girl, solved 9 − x = 5 by using a double sign-language counting procedure. She started by showing the sign-language number symbol for 9 on her left hand, and then started to count down in sign on the same hand (thus she was decreasing the initial quantity, 9, in the same way as it decreased in the story) and simultaneously counting up on her right (that is, keeping track on her right hand of the number of steps by which she was decreasing 9 to reach 5). When she had counted down to 5 on her left hand, she had the correct answer, 4, on her right hand (Frostad and Ahlberg, 1999: 290).

The example shows that once the child chose to represent the information as a signed number, she had to implement a counting procedure. In contrast, Anne, a 7-year-old girl, solved the problem $8 - x = 2$ using her fingers to represent objects. She extended 8 fingers, then explored how much had to be taken away from 8 to leave exactly 2 by folding different number of fingers, until she folded 6 fingers and saw that there were 2 still extended. She then counted the number of fingers she had folded. She was not counting down: she was treating the numbers as representations of the objects in the problem, and experimenting with 'taking away' until she had 2 fingers left.

Both of these solutions are informal and are analogous to the change in the story. But they use different procedures, because Pia is counting down and keeping track of the number of steps she has to count down to reach 5 whereas Anne is taking away individual representations for each object. Following Brissiaud (1992), Frostad and Ahlberg suggest that Anne is using analogue representations of cardinality whereas Pia is using a conventional representation in sign. Both children reach the correct solution in this case, but neither uses the sum that teachers would expect to see on paper: $9 - 5$ in Pia's problem and $8 - 2$ in Anne's problem.

Frostad and Ahlberg speculated that it is important for children to have experience with analogue representations in order to develop more flexible ways of representing the part–whole relations in additive reasoning problems. The children should be given the opportunity to do so in situations where the language is not a challenge for them, and use this strengthened understanding of part–whole relations as a basis for later linguistic representations of the problem. This suggestion contradicts teaching approaches that concentrate on the language of problems, textbooks, and paper and pencil tasks. This latter teaching strategy was found to be dominant in the teaching of deaf children in 1988 (Fridriksson and Stewart, 1988) and seems to have changed relatively little up to now (Kelly, Lang and Pagliaro, 2003).

To summarize: different ways of representing the numerical information in story problems influence hearing and deaf children's level of success. This difference is less important with the simplest type of change problem, where the type of change – increase or decrease – is directly represented by actions, counting procedures or arithmetic operations. However, in change-unknown and inverse problems, where the arithmetic operations are not a direct representation of the situation, children can be more successful if they use analogue representations for the numbers. With these, they can implement informal procedures that help them understand the relations in the problems better than when they use conventional number representations. It is speculated that children will improve in their

understanding of the basic part–whole logic through more experience
with problem-solving using analogue representations to analyse the logic
of the situation. This improved understanding of the logical relations
would result in later improvement in their problem-solving skills.

Helping deaf children represent sequences of events

Change problems involve a sequence of events and, as we have seen, deaf
children have difficulty with serial recall. It was suggested that deaf children could learn to use their superior spatial coding skills to represent
the sequences of events and thus improve their problem-solving skills.

We carried out two studies (Moreno, 1994; Nunes and Moreno, 2002)
where we attempted to draw on deaf children's special strength in spatial
representation in order to improve their problem-solving skill in change
problems. The first study was a short-term, focused intervention that considered only additive reasoning. It was thus possible to evaluate the
results of this intervention in the same focused manner, by giving children
assessments of their ability to solve additive reasoning problems. This
intervention and its evaluation will be presented in this chapter. The second project was a long-term one, where the children participated in a
variety of mathematical experiences especially designed for deaf pupils.
Accordingly, the evaluation of this second programme could not focus on
a single conceptual domain and was much broader. The activities
designed for intervention on additive reasoning will be described in this
chapter; the evaluation of the programme will be presented in Chapter 6.

The starting point for the first intervention study was the work of van
den Brink (1987), from the Freudenthal Institute in the Netherlands. The
institute has a well-known and highly respected programme of research
(including the design of teaching and assessments) in mathematics education. The core proposal in their teaching experiments, known as
Realistic Mathematics Education, is the idea that children should start
learning mathematics from situations that they can imagine and that make
sense to them (for a brief summary, see Gravemeijer, van den Heuvel and
Streefland, 1990). Children should be given the opportunity to create
their own problem-solving procedures and discuss a variety of routes to
solution, in order to learn to assess the efficacy and validity of different
procedures. In order to stimulate the children to imagine these situations,
drawings and diagrams are used both in teaching and in tests. This ample
use of visual material seemed appropriate for work with deaf children,
whose spatial skills are a strength to be capitalized on during instruction.

Van den Brink designed a situation – the bus story – that appeared to
offer an appropriate starting point for beginning the analysis of transformations. The preschoolers in his project were asked to imagine that one
of them was a bus driver and was driving past the different bus stops set

up in the classroom, picking up and dropping off passengers. This familiar situation was acted out, with the bus driver receiving a cap and
carrying a rope, which represented the bus. The children entered and left
the bus as the driver went around the room. The situation was later represented on the board, with magnetic figures being placed on a bus
drawing as they 'entered' the bus or taken away from the board as they
'left' the bus. The children then had the opportunity of drawing the bus
story and constructing their own bus problems, which they posed to each
other in the classroom. Figure 3.3 presents one child's drawing of a bus
story. It illustrates how the sequence of events – the bus stopped at different stops sequentially – was represented spatially by means of the
drawing of the bus route.

The children who took part in this project were five Year 2 children
(aged about 8 years), all attending a state-supported special school for the
deaf in London. They were matched in age and grade level to a group of
eight children attending another state-supported school for the deaf
in London. They were all severely or profoundly deaf and were being
educated in a total-communication environment. Moreno was a familiar
person to the children because she had carried out classroom observations in their classes previously.

The children were pre- and post-tested individually, and solved ten
story problems, which included both direct and inverse change problems.
The project children received four teaching sessions, delivered by the
teacher in the classroom as part of her regular mathematics teaching

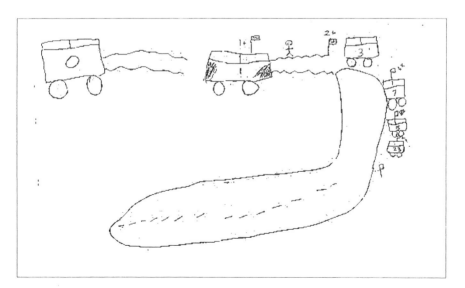

Figure 3.3 Drawing of a bus story by a deaf 7-year-old (reproduced from Moreno, 1994, with permission).

schedule. Thus they did not receive extra tuition but rather a focused tuition designed to use spatial coding to represent sequences of events. The sessions lasted for about one hour and were delivered approximately one week apart from each other. The post-test was administered the week after the intervention was concluded. The control children only responded to the pre- and post-test. The changes in the story problems in the pre- and post-test were about a variety of contents in the different stories; no story was about people entering and leaving buses. For example, an inverse change problem was: 'Yesterday a girl had some marbles. Today the girl gave 5 marbles to her friend. Now she has 8 marbles. How many marbles did she have yesterday?'

The teacher started with the bus story following van den Brink's acting out of the story, and then represented it on the board with a bus and magnetic figures of people. She then used other change story problems – first about people going in and out of a shop, then different types of change – which the children also represented through diagrams. She had a number line on the wall in her classroom, which the children sometimes used to discuss their answers, and she also made blocks available to the children to be used during problem-solving. The children solved the initial bus stories and then drew their own stories, creating problems for the other children to solve. As the teacher moved on to new problems, she continued to use the same approach: the children were asked to represent the changes spatially and also to create problems for their peers to solve. They checked their peers' solutions and discussed these with the whole class.

The children who participated in the project made significant progress in problem-solving from the pre- to the post-test. The control children did not show any change in the mean number of problems that they could solve correctly. Thus, although there was no increase in the amount of time used for teaching mathematics to the project children, they progressed significantly more than the control children in problem-solving within these 4 weeks.

Moreno observed some interesting discussions and insights that the deaf children had in the classroom. For example, one child spontaneously retraced the bus route from the end to the beginning, calculating how many people were in the bus before it stopped at the 8th, the 7th, the 6th stop etc. He then created a series of inverse problems for his peer by putting in his bus the total number of people at the end of the bus route and the changes that had occurred at each bus stop; he asked his peer how many people had entered the bus at the 1st stop. The peer was uncertain about what this meant so the child demonstrated with blocks how the solution was to apply the inverse operation.

Although the central idea in the design of this intervention was the use of spatial coding for sequences, it is not possible to attribute its success exclusively to this aspect of the intervention. Through the use of diagrams and the recognition of informal solution, these deaf children were now able to discuss their problem-solving procedures and probably develop a greater awareness of the part–whole logic in the course of these discussions. Previously they did not have these opportunities for discussion, because the teaching focused on the arithmetic operations and their answers were simply either right or wrong (i.e., they either had chosen the correct sum and done it correctly, or not). This is always the case when any educational innovation is introduced in the classroom; it is designed for one reason but it impacts the classroom in a number of ways. It is thus important to stress that the use of spatial codes was not the only thing that changed in the classroom: the opportunities for understanding the logical principles involved in change situations, the types of interactions that happened between peers and with the teacher, and most likely the level of motivation also changed. These factors and the specific effect of using spatial codes to represent sequences could only be isolated if the intervention had been carried out outside the classroom by a researcher. Thus further research is needed. Nevertheless, the results of this project are very encouraging and show that it is possible for teachers of the deaf to implement simple changes in the classroom that can have a positive impact on children's problem-solving skills.

In the second project, we (Nunes and Moreno, 2002) examined yet another way to represent sequential information through spatial relations, by providing the information in a cartoon format. Cartoons are part of children's experiences outside the classroom and they use spatial arrangements to represent sequences of events, so we expected that this would be a familiar experience.

Our project had two aims. The first was to give the deaf pupils opportunities to learn core mathematical concepts that many hearing pupils may learn informally outside school, and to promote connections between these informal concepts and the mathematical representations used in school. The second aim was to promote deaf pupils' access to information about word problems related to transformations over time by representing the problems through drawings and diagrams. As indicated earlier on, we did not carry out a separate analysis of the effects of the programme on additive reasoning; the evaluation of the effectiveness was based on a standardized test of mathematics achievement and thus more global than it is possible to discuss in this chapter. Thus examples of the tasks used in the programme will be presented but the assessment will be discussed in Chapter 6.

The programme was designed over a period of about 6 months through discussions with eight teachers of the deaf from different schools in London. Some teachers worked in mainstream schools with units for deaf children and some worked in special schools. The basic materials were designed by the researchers and discussed with the teachers before implementation. Each of the concepts to be taught was discussed during a special meeting, where the logical principles were analysed and the types of drawings and diagrams to be used were considered by the teachers. The materials were then revised to take into account their comments and prepared for delivery in the subsequent school terms.

The programme was delivered by six teachers to 23 children in their classrooms. They used their scheduled time for the teaching of mathematics to implement the programme and delivered it at their own pace over a period of about eight months; the teaching of additive reasoning lasted for about one month. The programme did not aim to replace the mathematics curriculum but to enhance the children's problem-solving experience. So most teachers used about one mathematics class a week to work on problem-solving using the programme materials.

All three types of change problems were included in the programme. The story problems were presented as cartoons, with the initial situation on the left, the change in the middle, and the final situation on the right. The children received booklets where they solved the problems. The booklets contained the illustrations but not the text of the problems, which was presented by the teacher using the usual means of communication employed in the classroom. Teachers were asked to encourage the children to resort to drawing and manipulative materials to help them think about the problems and to show how they solved the problems, even if they had used only written numbers in their problem-solving procedures.

The numerical information was presented in different ways, starting with drawings that represented the objects individually and, at later stages, using numbers and the number line. Following the indications of previous research (Frostad and Ahlberg, 1999), analogue number representations were used at the beginning of the programme to support children's thinking and talking about the part–whole relations. The use of different types of numerical representation simultaneously in later problems aimed at increasing the children's ability to establish connections between different types of representation, for example connecting analogue representations and the number line.

The figures (Figures 3.4 to 3.8) illustrate the resources used to present change problems. The idea of a number line was introduced to the children quite early on, by means of a problem about a board game (Figure 3.4). The board game makes it easy to discuss change-unknown and inverse problems and was used again later on in the programme. A change-unknown problem indicates where the player was and where the player is now; the child is asked to say what number the player got. The inverse problem indicates where the player is, and the last number the

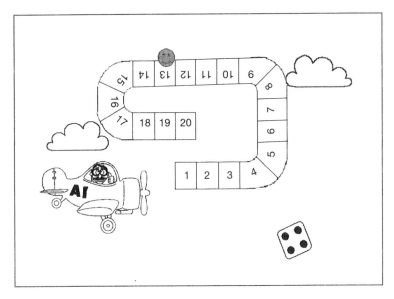

A girl was playing a game.

She was on the number 13.

She threw 4.

Where is she now?

Draw her counter on the right place.

Figure 3.4 A direct change problem used to introduce the idea of a number line.

player got; the child is asked to indicate where the player was before this turn. Pictures of a board game can also be produced for the children to create their own problems.

Figure 3.5 presents a direct problem and provides the children with a number line. This problem was included early on in the programme and had the aim of making the children familiar with using the number line to show what happened in the story.

Figures 3.6 and 3.7 present change-unknown problems. The children are also asked to provide different representations of the solution.

Figure 3.8 illustrates an inverse problem. When children demonstrate their solution using the number line, they can also discuss the part–whole relations and the need to apply the inverse operation to solve this problem by means of a sum.

Classroom observations showed that the children found it easy to approach the problems and enjoyed working with the booklets. In one class there was always a sort of celebration by the children when the teacher asked them to get the booklets. As observed in the intervention

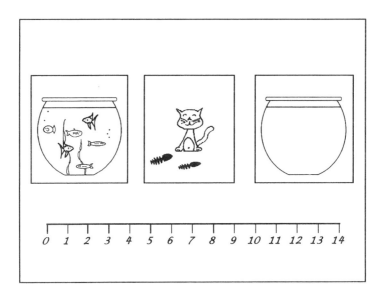

There were 6 fish in a bowl

The cat ate 2 fish

How many fish are in the bowl now?

Draw them in the empty bowl.

Show what happened in the story on the number line.

Figure 3.5 A direct change problem offering more practice with the number line.

using the bus story, the children became more active in designing their own problem-solving procedures, discussing them and creating their own problems for their peers to solve.

In summary, two ways were investigated of making use of deaf children's special strength with spatial coding to represent sequences of events. In the first one, the van den Brink bus story was the starting point. The children acted out a story, represented it on the board, and finally drew diagrams to represent the sequence of events in the bus story. They learned to use diagrams to represent a variety of problems and used different representations of the numerical information, including blocks, the number line, and signed and written conventional numbers. In the second project, the children were presented with cartoons that indicated sequences of events by means of spatial relations. They also worked with different types of number representations and learned to use their own diagrams to represent sequences of events. These experiences proved very effective in promoting the development of children's own methods,

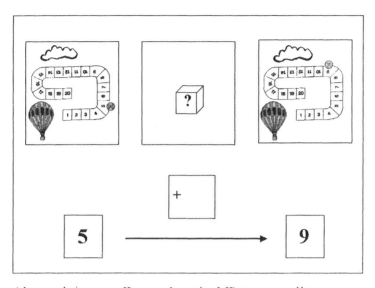

A boy was playing a game. He was on the number 5. His turn came and he got
a number. Now he is on the number 9. What number did he throw? Write your
answer in the box.

Figure 3.6 A change-unknown problem used to help connect the change with arithmetic operations.

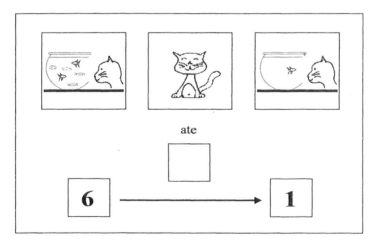

There were 6 fish in a bowl.
The cat ate some.
Now there is one fish.
How many fish did the cat eat?
Write the number in the box.
Is it add or take away? Write the number and sign in the box.

Figure 3.7 A change-unknown problem where the children are asked to indicate the
sign for the operation.

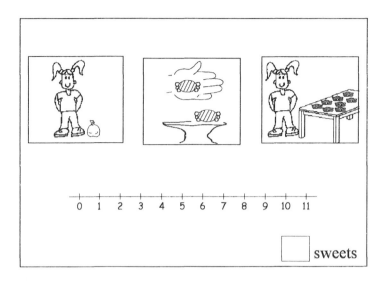

The girl had some sweets.
Her mum gave her 2 sweets.
Now she has 8 sweets.
How many sweets did she have in the bag?
Show what happened in the story on the number line.
Put your answer in the box.

Figure 3.8 Example of an inverse problem.

encouraging them to create spatial representations for problems, and creating opportunities for the children to explain their procedures and examine different ways of dealing with the part–whole logic. The teachers observed that the children spontaneously started to use drawings and diagrams in the course of their regular mathematics lessons, though they had not been instructed to do so. Thus the children felt that they could make use of their spatial coding skills to approach mathematical problems even when they were not directed to do so.

Situation type 2: combine problems

Some addition situations do not involve change but rather the combination of two sets, for example: 'Ron has 2 goldfish and 5 catfish. How many fish does he have in his bowl?' The difference between combine and change problems is subtle, but it does affect children's performance in some tasks. For example, young hearing children (aged 5 and 6) find it easier to understand the commutativity of addition in combine than in change problems. They realize that, if they are counting up to find the answer to the problem about Ron's fish, it does not matter whether they start counting up from 5 or from 2. In contrast, a considerable number of the same children think that in a change problem you must count up from the initial situation, or that you can't start from the value of the change and then add the initial situation on to it (Wright, 1994). However, there is no difference in hearing children's ability to solve combine and direct change problems: the percentage of correct responses for both problem types is quite high from the very beginning of primary school.

Our analysis of what makes story problems more difficult for deaf children than for hearing children leads to the expectation that combine problems are easier for deaf children than direct change problems. This hypothesis is based in the analysis of the processing demands of the two types of problems: direct change problems involve serial recall whereas combine problems do not. Combine problems are analogous to free recall tasks because the order in which one talks about the two sets does not matter. If this prediction is correct – that combine problems are easier than direct change problems for deaf children, though they are not for hearing children – our confidence in the analysis of why change problems are difficult for deaf children will be strengthened. This is a new prediction and one that focuses on a positive result for deaf children.

Hyde, Zevenbergen and Power (2003) recently provided evidence to support this hypothesis. The deaf children in their study were moderately to profoundly deaf students in their first to twelfth year in school in Queensland, Australia; information on age levels is not provided by the authors. All participants had basic English competency skills, as determined from school records and teacher judgements. The success rate for the deaf children in their study with combine problems was 67% in Year 1 and 83% in Year 2; from Year 3 on, it reached 100%. The success rate for direct change problems was also 67% in Year 1 but it did not increase as rapidly in the subsequent years: still 67% in Year 2, 86% in Year 3 and 75% in Year 4 (a small but insignificant drop in comparison to Year 3); it only reached 100% in Year 5. This difference does not appear in the results for hearing students, whose rate of correct response was slightly higher for change than for combine problems in Year 1 (90% correct for change and 79% for combine); for the subsequent school-year groups, there was no difference in the hearing children's performance across the two types of problems.

Combine problems can have two different types of structure: $a + b = x$ or $x + a = b$; for example: 'Ron has goldfish and catfish. He has 2 goldfish. Altogether he has 7 fish in his bowl. How many catfish does he have?' The description of the problem structure as $x + a = b$ or $a + x = b$ does not matter in the case of combine problems (as it does in the case of change problems), because combine problems do not involve a sequence of events.

In change-unknown problems, of the type a + x = b, children's informal strategies are to model the direction of the change – that is, increase the quantity by counting up – and keep track of the number of steps in this increase. This solution is not relevant here because there is no change in the quantity. So combine problems where one of the sets is not known should be more similar to inverse problems than to change-unknown problems. They should be more difficult than change-unknown problems because in combine problems there are no changes for the children to model. This is expected to be the case for both hearing and deaf children. And this is what Hyde, Zevenbergen and Power (2003) observed: whereas deaf children had some success in their first and second years in school with change-unknown problems, they showed no correct responses with inverse change and combine problems where one set is not known.

Helping deaf children represent combine problems with one set unknown

Nunes and Moreno (2002), concerned with the difficulty of combining problems where one set is not known, created different situations that helped

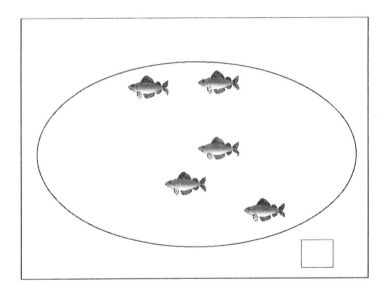

There are 11 fish in the pond.

You can see 5 of them.

Can you finish drawing the fish in the pond?

How many fish did you draw? Put your answer in the box.

Figure 3.9 A combine problem with a set unknown where the children can use drawing to find the answer.

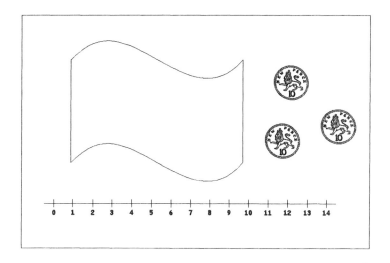

I have some 10p coins. You can see 3 of them. Nine are hidden under the cloth. Draw the number of coins that are under the cloth. How many coins do I have altogether?

Show how you solved the problem using the number line.

Figure 3.10 A hidden addend problem promoting the coordination between analogue representations through drawing and the number line.

the children find informal strategies in order to start making some sense of the meaning of these problems. Figures 3.9 to 3.12 display some examples.

Figure 3.9 presents an example used early on in the programme. Although the informal strategy of modelling the change does not apply to this type of problem, when the children are asked to complete the drawing they can use a similar strategy: count up from 5 until they reach 11, which is the number of fish in the pond, and then count the number of fish they drew.

The type of problem in Figure 3.10 has been extensively analysed by Steffe, Thompson and Richards (1982), who described children's informal problem-solving strategies. Because of the particular situation they describe – one set is hidden – they are known as hidden addend problems. Hearing children use counting to solve this problem: they tap on the box as if they were counting the hidden coins, and count up to the value of the set – nine in this case. Then they continue counting the visible coins. Our observations showed that hidden addend problems are difficult for deaf children and that, when they succeed, they use similar strategies of counting and pointing to invisible objects under the cloth. However, not all children discover this strategy. We encouraged them to

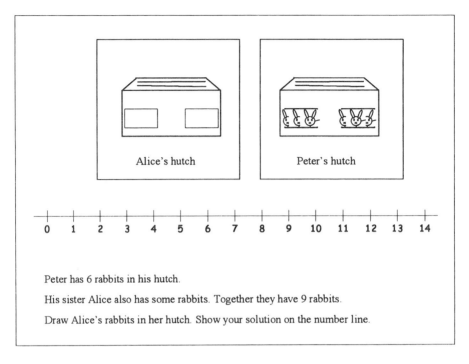

Peter has 6 rabbits in his hutch.

His sister Alice also has some rabbits. Together they have 9 rabbits.

Draw Alice's rabbits in her hutch. Show your solution on the number line.

Figure 3.11 A combine problem with a set unknown, to be solved with drawings and the number line.

imagine the hidden coins by drawing them and then count. This gives them a starting point for solving hidden addend problems.

Figure 3.11 shows the next step in helping the children build a solution: they can draw Alice's rabbits and then show how the solution works on the number line. It is expected that this spatial representation on the number line will support the children's understanding of how the part–whole logic works in this type of combine problem. Figure 3.12 shows a further example of combine problems with one set unknown. In the problem presented in Figure 3.11 the children are given the opportunity to combine the drawing with the number line, whereas in the problem in Figure 3.12 the explicit suggestion of drawing the toys is not made. If the children have understood the part–whole relations in the problem, they should be able to work out the solution on the number line.

The problem shown in Figure 3.12 proved quite useful in the classroom, because some children still drew the toys, some counted up from 2 using the number line, and others counted down from 12. Their discussion of the different procedures should be an important step in

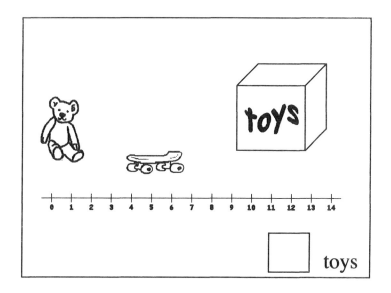

A boy has 12 toys altogether. You can see 2 of his toys.

How many toys are in the box?

Work it out on the number line.

Write your answer in the box.

Figure 3.12 A combine problem with a set unknown, to be solved with the support of the number line.

helping them become more aware of the connections between the different procedures and the part–whole logic.

In summary: simple combine problems are easier than direct change problems for deaf children because they do not require serial recall. Combine problems with one set unknown are considerably more difficult: they are similar to inverse change problems. It is possible to support the development of deaf children's informal strategies in combine problems with one set unknown by encouraging them to use drawings and the number line in order to understand better the part–whole relations in the story. The use of analogue representations through drawings helps them explore the part–whole relations; the combination of drawings and the number line supports the development of connections between different forms of numerical representation. The use of these spatial strategies also facilitates discussion, because the children can solve the problems and then compare their solutions. These discussions are expected to increase their awareness of the logic of part–whole relations.

Situation type 3: compare problems

There is no doubt amongst researchers that compare problems are the most difficult for all children. An example of a compare problem is: 'Jill has 2 books. Gail has 7 books. How many more books does Gail have than Jill?'

Compare problems, like change and combine problems, can have different structures but the differences cannot be represented using the same conventions as those for the other two problem types. The logic of the situation here is more complicated: there are two wholes in a compare problem and the question is which part of one whole cannot be set in correspondence with the other whole. The variations in the way the question can be asked are presented in Table 3.2.

Table 3.2 Different problem types in the compare situations

Difference unknown	
How many more?	Jill has 2 books. Gail has 7 books. How many more books does Gail have than Jill?
How many fewer (or less)?	Jill has 2 books. Gail has 7 books. How many fewer books does Jill have than Gail?
One whole unknown	
How many more?	Jill has 2 books. Gail has 5 books more than Jill. How many books does Gail have?
How many fewer (less)?	Gail has 7 books. Jill has 5 books fewer than Gail. How many books does Jill have?
Whole unknown; difference expressed in inverse form	
How many more?	Gail has 7 books. She has 5 books more than Jill. How many books does Jill have?
How many fewer (less)?	Jill has 2 books. She has 5 books fewer than Gail. How many books does Gail have?

An analysis of Table 3.2 will quickly convince the reader of the complexity of different types of compare problems. It is clear that the easiest problems are those where the words 'more' and 'less' coincide with a correct answer obtained by means of addition or subtraction, respectively. But this is not sufficient to help anticipate the level of difficulty of compare problems. The first two problems in the table generate many mistakes, although in the second problem, where the question is 'How many fewer?', the correct answer would be obtained by subtraction. In this problem, the most frequent error observed among both hearing and deaf children is to say the number of books owned by Jill, who has fewer books. In the first problem, the most common error is to say the number of books owned by Gail, who has more books. These answers suggest that the children do not see that any arithmetic operation is called for in this problem.

At later ages, children shift to adding when the problem asks 'How many more?' and subtracting when the problem asks 'How many fewer?'. However, these correct responses do not necessarily indicate comprehension, and may be the product of a strategy where the child matches the operation to a word, for lack of a better strategy.

It does not seem necessary to discuss the different rates of correct responses for hearing and deaf pupils in these problems; the reader is referred to Hyde, Zevenbergen and Power (2003) for this information. All problem types were more difficult for the deaf than for the hearing children in their study. Deaf children in their third year in primary school still showed no success in four of the six types of compare problems. At the end of primary school, only one-third of the responses to the same four problems were correct. This compares poorly with hearing children's performance, whose success rate in the same problems varied between 67% and 96% correct at the end of primary school.

Working with more complex compare problems, Kelly, Lang, Mousley and Davis (2002) report that deaf college students enrolled in first-year algebra courses at the National Technical Institute for the Deaf (Rochester Institute of Technology, New York) still have difficulty with the relational expressions used in compare problems. There is thus no doubt that compare problems are challenging for deaf pupils.

One reason why this may be so is the focus placed on language in the problem-solving instruction designed for deaf pupils. An analysis of Table 3.2 will show that there is no simple connection between particular linguistic expressions in the problems and the procedures that can lead to successful solution.

Helping deaf children represent compare problems

In our programme (Nunes and Moreno, 2002) there was no attempt to design instruction that focused on the language used in compare problems. The aim of the programme was to help the children use analogue representations of number in order to explore the part–whole logic that is required for a sound approach to solution. The same strategy used for combine and change problems was employed: the problems were presented through drawings; the children were encouraged to use a variety of numerical representations in problem-solving; their strength with spatial coding was brought into play; and there was encouragement for discussing different procedures. Some examples of comparison problems are presented in Figures 3.13 to 3.16.

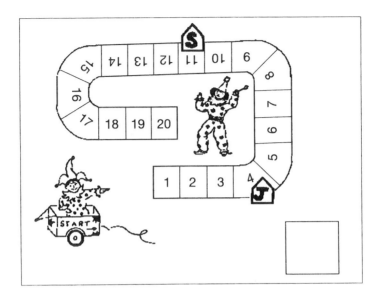

Jamal and Serena are playing a game.

Jamal is at number 4. Serena is at number 11.

Serena is winning. How many squares ahead is Serena?

Put your answer in the box.

Figure 3.13 An introduction to compare problems through a board game.

Comparing Serena's and Jamal's positions in the board game (Figure 3.13) is a useful start: the children can make a connection between the difference in their places on the board and the number that Jamal has to move on in order to catch up with Serena. This introduces the idea that some action is required in the comparison between Jamal's and Serena's positions on the board.

The problem shown in Figure 3.14 also introduces the idea of a connection between change problems and compare problems, and thus helps the children think of part–whole relations in the context of compare problems. Nunes and Bryant (1991, 1996) have shown that hearing children aged 6 or 7 years make substantial improvements in compare problems when they are taught using examples such as the one in Figure 3.14. So it was reasoned that deaf children might also benefit from working with this type of question.

The problem in Figure 3.14 shows how the spatial cues used in the comparison between the boy's and the girl's stickers can be transferred to the number line and used in other types of problems and with other displays.

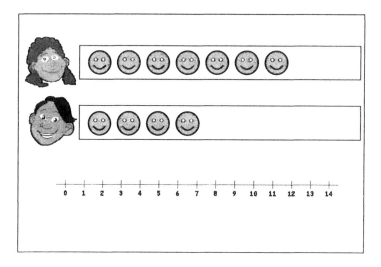

The girl had 7 stickers for good behaviour. The boy also had 7 stickers.

The boy behaved very badly today so the teacher took some of his stickers away. How many stickers did the teacher take away? How many less stickers does the boy now have than the girl?

Show your answers on the number line.

Figure 3.14 A compare problem solved through an easier question: how many do we have to give to the boy so he has the same number as the girl?

Classroom observations showed that the children were able to use the spatial cues and engaged in discussions about the procedures and part–whole relations when solving these problems.

Summary and conclusions

The traditional approach to teaching addition and subtraction story problems has been to classify these problems in terms of the *procedures* used to solve them, addition or subtraction. This classification does not shed light on why some problems are considerably more difficult than others, even if they could be solved by the same sum.

Research in the last two or three decades has provided an alternative to the teaching of story problems, by offering classifications that consider the logic of the problem, the types of situation involved, and the resources used in the representation of the problem information. This research led to the clarification of the logic in additive reasoning, which is based on part–whole relations. Three types of situation involving

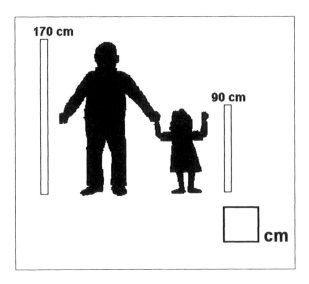

Daddy and Claire are measuring themselves on their height charts.

They have two height charts that are the same height as they are.

Daddy's height chart is 170 cm long. Claire's height chart is 90 cm long.

Daddy is taller. How much taller is he? Write your answer in the box.

Figure 3.15 A compare problem with large numbers, using spatial representation.

part–whole relations are distinguished: change, combine and compare situations. In each of these situations, the problem structure can vary, making the problem easier or more difficult for the children. This analysis proved to be of considerable use for understanding why deaf children find some additive reasoning situations more difficult than others.

First, it was shown that change problems require serial recall. In non-computational change problems that do not require inferences, and so pose task demands that deaf children can cope with, there is no difference between deaf and hearing children's performance. In change problems, where there is an increase in task demands because of the need to make an inference, deaf children's performance is weaker than that of hearing children, even if the problem is non-computational. The increased task demands of inverse and change-unknown problems make these significantly more difficult for the deaf children than for the hearing children. But there are ways of helping deaf children cope with these increased task demands. They can learn to code sequences of events using their strong spatial skills. Programmes that have used such methods and allowed the children to represent the numerical information in different ways – in an analogue manner as well as using a number line

The girl is 8 years old.
There are 8 candles on her cake.
She is 3 years older than the boy.
Can you draw the boy's candles on his cake?
Show the girl's and the boy's ages on the number line.

Figure 3.16 A compare problem where analogue representations of number are used and then coordinated with the number line

and conventional signs – had a significant effect on deaf pupils' problem-solving skills.

A second research result of importance was the demonstration that deaf children, even at the beginning of school, have informal strategies for solving problems and can use them as effectively as hearing children to solve combine problems. Because combine problems do not require serial recall, as change problems do, the deaf children's good performance is a demonstration that they have sufficient number understanding to succeed when they can cope with the task demands. The difficulty of combine problems with one set unknown is similar to that of inverse problems for both hearing and deaf pupils because the informal strategies they use are not effective here. Instruction that helps deaf children to analyse this type of problem in terms of part–whole relations has a positive effect on their problem-solving.

Finally, compare problems were analysed. These are difficult for hearing children but significantly more so for deaf children. Strategies developed for supporting hearing children's understanding of compare problems can also be effective with deaf children.

It is possible to conclude this chapter with a positive message. The analysis of deaf children's strengths and difficulties was fruitful in helping us understand why deaf children have greater difficulty than hearing children with some types of story problems. The research reviewed does not lead to the conclusion that deaf children's difficulties are essentially with number understanding – they perform as well as hearing children when they can cope with the task demands. Thus this chapter shows a path to improve their problem-solving skills, and presents some significant findings that show that this path is effective.

CHAPTER 4

Reading and writing numbers

One of the important aims of schools in the first years is to teach children how to read and write words as well as numbers. Learning to read and write words is a major challenge for deaf children. English uses an alphabetic writing system, which means that letters represent the sounds in words. Severely and profoundly deaf children have no direct experience of speech sounds and this makes learning to read and write words very difficult for them.

Learning to read and write numbers is very different from reading and writing words. The digits 1, 2, 3 etc. do not represent the sounds in the words one, two, three etc. They represent a quantity, a value. This could make learning to read and write numbers easier for deaf children than reading and writing words. But this is not an easy task, either for hearing or for deaf children. Written numbers involve logic and conventions, and children must understand the logic and learn the conventions in order to read and write numbers.

This chapter considers first the logic of writing numbers in the Hindu-Arabic number system that we use. In the second main section, the issues related to learning the conventions are analysed. The final section considers whether learning the logic of our number system matters for learning to read and write numbers and for mathematics learning in general.

The logic of our number system: the concepts of units of different values and additive composition

We regularly use two number systems – one that is oral or signed, depending on our first language, and a second that is written. In Chapter 2, oral and signed numbers were referred to as counting systems. Counting systems, it was argued, have an organization; the numbers are not remembered as entities entirely independent of each other – there are rules that allow us to generate these numbers. In this chapter it will be argued that there is a logical property of numbers, named additive composition, which is implicit in counting systems. It is important for children to

ze why additive composition is implicit in this number:
twenty-one is the sum of twenty plus one. It is quite possible that children
do not think at all about additive composition when learning to count in
English up to twenty. There are no clear cues to additive composition in
the counting string up till then. But after twenty, when the composition
of decades with units is discernible in the counting string, children have
good reasons to start thinking of the idea of additive composition. It is
possible that children learn both rules for forming number labels and also
something about additive composition when they count on after twenty.

A second concept implicit in our numeration system is the idea of units
of different values. We count ones until we form a group of ten ones; then
we count tens, which is a different-sized unit, and ones; when we form a
group of ten tens, we start counting hundreds, tens and ones, and so on.
This concept is crucial to understanding written numbers because the
same digit in a different position in a written number indicates a different-
sized unit: in 48 the 4 indicates the number of tens, so it stands for the
value 40, whereas in 64 the 4 indicates the number of ones, so it indicates
the value 4.

In school much time is spent teaching hearing as well as deaf children
the conventions for this representation – that is, teaching them that the
place where the digit is indicates its value. It is recognized that our place-
value system cannot be understood without these concepts. We know that
children often learn informally about many concepts that they are taught
later in school, and that this informal learning is crucial to their later
learning in school. So it is fair to ask whether children have some informal learning about the concept of units of different values before they are
taught these ideas in school. Do they have informal experiences that help
them understand the concepts implicit in our number system? Do hearing and deaf children have the same informal knowledge of these
concepts when they reach school? Some answers to these questions are
considered in this first section of the chapter.

Counting with different types of units: the Shop Task

Some time ago, we (Nunes Carraher, 1982, 1985; Nunes Carraher and
Schliemann, 1990) developed an assessment of children's understanding
of the concept of units and additive composition, which is known as the

Shop Task. In the Shop Task, the children are invited to play a pretend-shop game, where the researcher is the seller and the child is the buyer. The children are given two types of items: one type focuses only on the understanding of units, while the second type focuses on additive composition.

Assessing children's understanding of units

The researcher sets out some sweets for the shop and gives the child some pretend coins – which are tokens of different colours, with particular colours representing particular values. We have carried out the task with real coins on some occasions but this proves to be more distracting and no easier for the children, so normally we use pretend coins on the Shop Task. The children do not find it difficult to memorize the conventions – for example, yellow is 1p and blue is 5p. The conventions are introduced as the task progresses, so that at any time the children only have to think of the values that are being used on the task – typically two values. These pretend coins will be referred to as coins from now on.

In order to test the children's understanding of the concept of units, the researcher asks the child to set out a number of coins in a row; for example, five 1p coins. The researcher then sets out a row of five 5p coins, and ensures that the child remembers that yellow tokens are 1p each and blue tokens are 5p each. The researcher then tells the child: 'Imagine you had these coins [showing one of the rows] and another girl/boy had these coins [showing the other row], and you two went to the shop to buy sweets. You both spend all your money on these sweets. Will you be able to buy the same amount of sweets?' If the child understands the idea of different units, the child would be able to tell that the one with five 5p coins would be able to buy more sweets. The child should be able to conclude this even if he/she cannot count the money in fives. If the child does not understand the idea of units, the child would think only of the number of coins and think that the children would be able to buy the same amount of sweets.

We gave this task to hearing preschoolers and unschooled adults in Brazil (Nunes Carraher, 1985; Nunes and Bryant, 1996), who had never been taught to write and read numbers. If they had had informal experiences that could help them understand the concept of units, they would be able to provide the correct answer to this question. All the unschooled adults and 60% of the preschool children had no hesitation in indicating that the child with more valuable coins would be able to buy more sweets. David Wood (personal communication) has since used this task in his investigations and also found that about 60% of the hearing 5-year-olds in England succeed on this task. This allows us to say with some confidence that hearing children do have access to the concept of units through their informal experiences – most likely with money but perhaps also in other situations.

Moreno (2000) gave this task to 69 hearing schoolchildren aged 7 and 8 years in England. None had any difficulty with the task. So we can conclude that if hearing children have not yet developed the concept of units of different sizes before school, they clearly do so in the first 2 years.

We (Nunes and Moreno, 1998a) gave this task to 80 deaf children who were attending Years 2 through to 5 in school. There were approximately 20 children in each school year. Some of the children ($n = 24$) were in special schools for the deaf and were users of BSL; the remaining children ($n = 56$) were attending mainstream schools and were either in oral education or total-communication programmes. The deaf children showed much less success on this task than hearing children. The percentage of children in each year group who answered this question correctly is shown in Table 4.1. The table shows that even in Year 5 there were still 2 out of 24 children who did not succeed on this task.

Table 4.1 Percentage of children who succeeded in the Concept of Units Task by type of education (total number of children in brackets)

Year group	BSL education	Oral or total communication
2	100 ($n = 4$)	80 ($n = 15$)
3	75 ($n = 4$)	67 ($n = 15$)
4	100 ($n = 4$)	87 ($n = 14$)
5	92 ($n = 12$)	92 ($n = 12$)
	$N = 24$	$N = 56$

It would have been useful to carry out a comparison between the children whose parents are deaf and who were exposed to BSL from birth and those who were born to hearing parents. It is often argued that deaf children of deaf parents have a richer exposure to a variety of situations, developing their understanding of the world more quickly than deaf children of hearing parents. It would be very good to know whether this applies to their understanding of the idea of units. Because only 10 of the children had deaf parents and fewer used BSL as their first language (some of the deaf parents had been educated orally and learned BSL at a later age), it was not possible to carry out this comparison. We analysed instead whether BSL had an influence on the children's success in the Units Task. Table 4.1 separates out the children by the type of education they were receiving. BSL education is contrasted with oral or total communication. There is a slightly higher tendency for the children educated in BSL to succeed on this task. However, a statistical analysis that tested for a greater likelihood of being successful on the task if the child is a BSL user, after controlling for year group in school, did not show any significant differences between the two groups. So we cannot conclude that education in BSL has an effect on the level of success on this task.

These results suggest that deaf children enter school with less informal knowledge of the concept of units than hearing children. This would place at a disadvantage those deaf children who lack this informal concept. Is there any way that schools can provide experience to help children develop the concept of units of different sizes?

Helping children understand the concept of units of different sizes

The logical principle that is relevant to the understanding of units of different sizes is the idea of one-to-many correspondences. If the children can understand that for each 1p coin in one row there would be five 1p coins in the other row, they would realize that there is more money in the row with 5p coins. How can we help children understand this?

Frydman and Bryant (1988) created a task that can be used to improve hearing children's understanding of the concept of units. They asked 4- and 5-year-olds to share out pretend sweets to two bears. But these bears were very fussy. One bear only liked his sweets in single units – represented in their task by single Unifix blocks. The other bear only liked his sweets in double units – represented by two Unifix blocks glued together. The children's task was to carry out a distribution of sweets respecting the bears' preferences and making sure that the distribution was fair: both bears had to receive the same amount of sweets to eat.

The 4-year-olds found this task very difficult: they used a sharing procedure of one-for-this-bear-and-one-for-that-bear, thus giving a double sweet to one bear every time they gave a single sweet to the other. They quickly realized that this was not ending up in a fair share, but did not know how to fix it. The 5-year-olds were actually very good at this task.

In order to help the 4-year-olds, Frydman and Bryant made a change to their task. In their original task, all the Unifix blocks had been of the same colour. They changed the task so that now the double blocks were made of one yellow brick and one blue brick, helping the children code the fact that these blocks were double through more visual information. The single blocks available were also yellow and blue. This meant that the children could give a double sweet to one bear and then a single of each colour to the other bear, thus finding a visual path to maintaining the fairness of the distribution. Frydman and Bryant observed that the 4-year-olds immediately improved their distribution procedure when they could use this visual information, and produced as many fair distributions as the 5-year-olds. Furthermore, when they later returned to the original situation, where all the bricks were of the same colour, they continued to be able to produce fair distributions. They had learned to solve this one-to-many correspondence problem where one bear gets one double unit while the other gets two single units.

In a later study, one of my colleagues (Wang, 1995) investigated whether children's performance on the task developed by Frydman and Bryant was related to their ability to distribute money fairly. The children had to give out the same amount of money to two dolls, who were just as fussy as the bears: one doll only liked 1p coins and the other only liked 2p coins. The difference between the tasks is that the children have analogue representations in the bear task: a double sweet is represented by two sweets glued together, which can be identified as two. In the coins task, the representation is symbolic: the number 2 on the coin represents its value as 2p. The distinction between analogue and symbolic representations was introduced in Chapter 3, where it was argued that analogue representations facilitate the use of informal and visual strategies.

Wang found that children perform better on the task of the bears with the sweets than on the task of the dolls with the coins. Thus it is easier for preschool children to use analogue than symbolic representations of units of different sizes. However, practice in the bears task improved their performance in the dolls task. Having worked on a task where they could code the double units visually, they could perform better in a task where the double units are represented symbolically.

Although these studies were carried out with hearing children, it is reasonable to expect that deaf children will also find it easier to solve problems when they are given an analogue representation of the different sizes of the units than when they are given problems with a symbolic representation. The difference between the two conditions may be even more noticeable with deaf preschoolers, who have better visual representation skills than hearing children (see Chapter 2). But it must be stressed that the interventions to help the deaf children should have the aim of supporting the transition from analogue to symbolic representation: the proof of the pudding will be whether they can develop a solid understanding of the concept of units when these are represented symbolically in written numbers. So it is suggested that, in order to help the deaf children develop the concept of units, they should have experience with the three types of situations described in the preceding paragraphs.

In summary, the concept of units of different sizes seems to be developed by hearing children informally, often before school. Deaf children's performance on this type of task shows a significant delay. This means that they are likely to be at a disadvantage when learning about the number system in school. Hearing children perform better on tasks that involve the concept of units when the tasks are presented to them using analogue rather than symbolic representations (Frydman and Bryant, 1988; Wang, 1995). If the children can code visually that a double unit is made of two singles, they understand better that these double units correspond to two single units. Practice in solving problems in situations where this visual coding is facilitated improves the performance of hearing 4-year-olds; this improvement transfers to later tasks, where the visual coding is no longer facilitated. So it is hypothesized that practice in problem-solving of the same type would benefit deaf children's understanding of units. Although research with deaf children is still lacking in this type of teaching situation, it is encouraging to know that deaf children are very good at using visual codes and are likely to learn about units of different sizes if given the right type of problem-solving experience.

Assessing children's understanding of additive composition

After testing children's understanding of units in the pretend shop, we presented the children with items that assessed their understanding of additive composition. More objects were placed on the table along with the sweets – paper clips, pens, pencils, erasers and a variety of small toys. On different trials, the children were given different combinations of coins to carry out their purchases. We used four types of trials: (1) trials where they only had 1p coins; (2) trials where they had one 5p and four 1p coins; (3) trials where they had one 10p and nine 1p coins; and (4) trials where they had one 20p and nine 1p coins.

The first type of trial works only as a control: when counting 1p coins, the children do not need to use the concept of additive composition. These trials help us to find out whether the child knows how to count to a given number. The additive composition items presented to the children are always with values within their counting range.

The other types of trials are used to assess the children's understanding of additive composition: for example, when the children are given one 5p and four 1p coins and asked to pay 7p for a pencil, they will have to use a combination of 5p plus two 1p coins. Thus this requires the children to understand that the number 7 can be formed by 5 + 2. Similarly, when the children are asked to pay 13p using a combination of 10p and 1p coins, the children can only solve the problem if they understand that 13 can be formed by 10 + 3. When they are asked to pay 21p using a mixture of 20p and 1p coins, they can only solve the item if they understand that 21 is the same as 20 + 1.

Our findings about hearing children's understanding of additive composition are very clear. We present them here and compare them with results obtained with the 80 deaf children who participated in our study.

First, hearing children who fail the task on the concept of units do not perform well on the additive composition items. Thus, although the children know the counting sequence and are able to count 'five, six, seven' using 1p coins, if they do not understand the concept of units, they do not think of taking the 5p coin and counting on 'six, seven', to pay 7p in the Shop Task. This is also true of deaf children. We divided the deaf children into two groups, one formed by the children who had failed the Concept of Units Task and the other formed by the children who had been successful on the same task. Out of a total number of 8 items, the mean number of correct responses was 2.8 for the children who failed the units task and 4.8 for the children who had been successful on the units task. The difference between the two groups was statistically significant ($F_{1,80} = 3.89$; $p = 0.05$). This suggests that both hearing and deaf children should have the opportunity to learn about units of different sizes before they are given instruction on additive composition.

Second, hearing children aged 7 or 8 have no difficulty with additive composition on the Shop Task (Moreno, 2000; Nunes and Bryant, 1996). In contrast, deaf children in this age range find the additive composition task challenging. Half of the children in Years 2 and 3 (average age 6 years 10 months and 8 years 6 months, respectively) did not pass any of the eight additive composition items and only 25% obtained a full score. There was a huge change in Years 4 and 5, when 60% and 70%, respectively, obtained a full score on the additive composition items, and only 10% had no points on this task. The progress with schooling was statistically significant ($F_{3,78} = 7.62$; $p < 0.001$). However, these results show a considerable delay in comparison with hearing children's performance and indicate that it is very important that deaf children should receive instruction on additive composition in school. There was no difference in the children's performance on this task as a function of the language used in their education, BSL versus oral or total communication.

Third, hearing children perform better on items where they have to compose values with a 20p coin and 1p coins than in smaller values, where they have to combine 5p with 1p, or 10p with 1p coins. The reason for this better performance seems to be the transparency of the language with respect to the concept of additive composition. When we say in English 'pay twenty-three pence', the expression 'twenty-three' gives a clue to the choice of a 20p coin plus three 1p coins. In contrast, there is no such clue when we say 'pay seven' and the children have to use one 5p and two 1p coins. Similarly, there is no clear linguistic cue to additive composition in the expression 'pay thirteen'. So hearing children perform better when there is support from the linguistic cues to facilitate the use of additive composition. This effect of linguistic cues is noted not only in English but also in other languages (see Miura, Kim, Chang and Okamoto, 1988; Miura et al., 1994; Nunes and Bryant, 1996).

To test whether deaf children seem to use linguistic cues on the Shop Task, we separated the children into two groups, one group composed of children being educated in BSL and the second group composed of children being educated orally or in a total-communication school. In both English and BSL, there are more cues to additive composition after the number 20, but these cues are different. In English, the word for 21 indicates that there is a decade, twenty, and a single unit, one. In BSL, the number 21 is signed as 2 and 1, with a spatial representation that might be taken by the children to indicate decades or not – the number 2 is signed to the left of the number 1. Our question was whether one system – English or BSL – gives the children a better cue to the idea of additive composition than the other.

In Table 4.2 the mean number of correct responses that the children gave to each of the three types of items is presented separately by the children's language of education. For both groups, the children's performance was very similar across the three types of items and there is no sign of linguistic facilitation in the combinations using 20. This result leads to the speculation that the deaf children were not using linguistic cues as much as hearing children when solving this task. If they had been using language, then at least those children who were being educated in English should have found the task with 20p coins easier.

Table 4.2 Mean number correct for three types of additive composition items by language used in school

Year group	BSL education	Oral or total communication
Combining 5p and 1p	1.3	1.2
Combining 10p and 1p	1.2	1.0
Combining 20p and 1p	1.1	1.0
	$N = 24$	$N = 56$

Fourth, we presented two types of additive composition items to the children: (1) the 'pay x' items, described previously, where the child is asked to pay for a pretend purchase; and (2) the 'money counting' task, where the researcher changes roles with the child and carries out a pretend purchase, paying the child a certain amount and asking the child to count how much money the researcher has given him/her. The same types of items are given in this money-counting task: combinations of 5p and 1p, 10p and 1p, and 20p and 1p coins. The reason for using this second task is that it is possible for the researcher to try to influence the performance of the children who failed in the 'pay x' task and see whether the children make progress.

Psychologists use the method of giving the children hints, and observing how the children use the hints provided to them, in order to test what sort of hint helps children who initially failed the task. This method is known in psychology as *micro-genetic analysis*. Micro-genetic analysis tests the possible causes or origin (i.e., the genesis) of success: if the children can use a hint and succeed on the task, then it is possible that this hint plays a role in helping the children to understand the concept.

Hearing and deaf children's mistakes in the 'pay x' task are very similar. Most often, they count all the coins as if they were 1p coins – even if the researcher reminds them of the value of the other coins. For example, when the children are given one 5p coin and four 1p coins and asked to pay 7p, they count all the coins as if they were 1p coins and conclude that they do not have enough money to pay 7p. Their counting stops at five. If the researcher simply insists with them that the 5p coin should be counted as 'five', they can end up with a count that is disconnected: they will say 'five', while pointing to the 5p coin, and count to four while pointing to the 1p coins, and will not know how to put the two together.

In the money-counting task, we give the children the coins and ask them how much money we have given them. The items presented are of the same type that the child failed in the 'pay x' task. For example, we can give the children one 5p and three 1p coins and ask how much money we have given them. We observed that some hearing and deaf children who fail the 'pay x' task can succeed in this money-counting task by using a particular gesture when counting. They tap five times on the 5p coin, counting to five, and then go on to tap on each 1p coin, and obtain the correct count. Their gesture of tapping five times on the coin changes the symbolic representation offered by the coin into an analogue representation created by the child: they point five times to the coin as if there were five things there. Using this resource, they can go on and count the total correctly. The gestures used by the children suggested to us that, in order to help them understand additive composition, we should suggest to them the use of analogue representations. We then tested the idea of the use of analogue representations in a variety of situations – first through micro-genetic analysis and later during the intervention study, which was mentioned in Chapter 3. But before moving on to describing these studies, one more word should be said about these analogue representations where children point repeatedly to one object while counting.

Steffe, Thompson and Richards (1982) also described children's use of analogue representations through tapping when they were solving hidden addend problems, as mentioned earlier on.

Later research by one of my colleagues, Kornilaki (1994), showed that only children who were able to solve hidden addend problems succeeded on the additive composition task – but that not all of the children who passed the hidden addend problem also passed the additive composition task. This is intriguing because the same type of gesture can be used in both tasks. Why do the children fail to use on the Shop Task a method that helped them in the hidden addend task? Kornilaki thought that this might be due to the hints already present in the situations. In the hidden addend task, the sweets are placed in the box and the children can more easily imagine their analogue representation. On the Shop Task, the coins represent values without such cues.

What can we conclude from these findings? One possible conclusion is that the tapping gesture or the use of fingers, which help the children replace the symbolic representation with an analogue one, must be a transitional behaviour, important when the children are still facing difficulties with additive composition. This transitional behaviour can be abandoned later, when they become able to go straight to the solution. The second conclusion is that, if the situation does not give the children cues to the use of analogue representations, which would help them solve the problem, the researcher might be able to give the child such cues.

Having stressed the importance of analogue representations as transitional behaviours, we can now turn to how this can be done.

Promoting deaf children's understanding of the additive composition

In our investigations, we used two methods to see whether these representations help. The first was a micro-genetic analysis of work carried out with two deaf children. The second was the design of tasks that can be used in the classroom.

The micro-genetic study involved two deaf children who had scored 1 and 2, respectively, on the eight additive composition items in the Shop Task. One child was in Year 3 (aged 9) and the other was in Year 5 (aged 11). Each child was seen individually. Because the children's behaviour was very similar, only the behaviour of the second one, who was in Year 5, is described here.

A row with one 5p and four 1p coins was placed in front of the child and he was asked to count how much money I had given him.

Researcher (TN):	How much money did I give you?
Child:	Five (pointing to the 5p coin), one, one, one.
TN:	And if you put them together, how much is it?
Child:	[Offers several answers, seeming to be trying out different ideas as the researcher shows the coins and asks the question] Fifty p. One pound. One pound fifty. [Then the researcher intervenes.]
TN:	Show me with your fingers, show me five fingers.
Child:	(Shows correctly.)

TN:	And one more?
Child:	(Puts one more finger up, looks at both hands but does not answer.)
TN:	How many fingers now?
Child:	Six.
TN:	That's right, six. Can you do that with the money?
Child:	That's five (showing the 5p coin).
TN:	Five.
Child:	One (showing the 1p coin).
TN:	Yes, five with a one, makes what?
Child:	(With a smile, as if he had made a sudden discovery) Six!
TN:	Yes, go on. With this one?
Child:	(Goes on to count the other two coins) Seven, eight, nine. Nine p!
TN:	(Gets back to the shopping situation and asks the child to choose something to buy. He chooses a balloon.) That costs 7p.
Child:	(Takes a 1p and a 5p coin.) One p, five p.
TN:	And together, that makes what?
Child:	One p and five p again (raises his fingers), one p and five p, six p.
TN:	That's right. But you need seven p.
Child:	Six p, seven p (taking a 1p coin) – seven p!
TN:	[Changes the task] Now I am giving you one 10p coin and these 1p coins (six 1p coins). How much money do you have now?
Child:	That's a ten p (shows ten fingers), that's a one p (shows the coin).
TN:	That's right.
Child:	(Counts his fingers one by one, as if he did not know how many fingers he has, then points to one more finger but stops counting.)
TN:	And one more?
Child:	(Hesitates) Eleven! (Again with a smile as if he had made a discovery.)
TN:	That's right, that's very good. How much money do you have?
Child:	(Points again to the 10p and the 1p coin) Eleven p!
TN:	Yes, that's right. What about the rest?

Child:	[Counts on] Twelve, thirteen, fourteen, fifteen, seventeen p [skips sixteen, gives seventeen as the answer].

This micro-genetic approach was only tried out with two children. In both cases, the children found it quite easy to pursue the correct count after using the analogue representation with fingers side by side with the symbolic representation for the coin. The older child, in Year 5, seems to have grasped the idea immediately and transferred it from the 5p to the 10p coin without difficulty. He then went on to count combinations of 20p and 1p coins without hesitation. The younger one, in Year 3, required prompting to make the change from the situation with 5p to the one with 10p. But once he had used the analogue representation with the 10p coin once, he did not find it difficult to proceed to the other items, and went on to solve the 20p items without hesitation.

Because we only worked with two children using this method, we cannot give quantitative information regarding how many children find this use of analogue representations easy. It can only be hypothesized that deaf children will be able to use this method – which is used spontaneously by some hearing and deaf children to solve the task – and build the concept of additive composition. However, it is not suggested that one trial on one day will be sufficient. Previous research shows that children can take steps forward when working with the support of a tutor but might take steps backwards in the absence of support. So it might be necessary for teachers to stimulate the pupils to use analogue representations when they show difficulties with symbolic representation more than once in the context of additive composition. For this reason, we developed different paper and pencil tasks, using the number line – which works as an analogue representation – but also other resources. The tasks include both hidden addend problems and items from the Shop Task. Some examples are presented in Figures 4.1 to 4.6.

After this discussion of the logic that is involved in reading and writing numbers, we turn now to an analysis of how children learn the conventions of our place-value system.

Learning place-value conventions

One of the hypotheses that has been considered by researchers is that children learn to read and write numbers by making a direct connection between oral and written numbers, without the participation of logic. In the case of deaf children who sign, they would make a direct connection between signed and written numbers. Unfortunately, this simple idea does not work, as will be shown in the course of this section. The evidence that

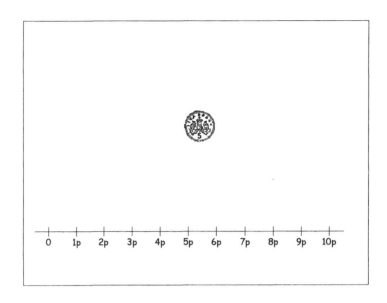

Here is a coin. The number line shows the values up to 10p.
Show on the number line the value of this coin.

Figure 4.1 An item used to help the children coordinate the symbolic
representation of a 5p coin with its analogue representation on the number line.

will be presented in this chapter suggests quite a different picture – that
logic matters. Most of the research reviewed here was carried out with
hearing children. There is a paucity of research with deaf children, especially with children who sign, but a study of children using Catalan Sign
Language (CSL), which is described in some detail later on, will shed some
light on the connection between signed and written numbers. This
research will provide important evidence to show that the connection
between signed numbers, and reading and writing numbers, is not so
direct.

Even before children are taught how to read and write numbers, they
start to form ideas about how written numbers are put together. Kamii
(1980) and Sinclair and Sinclair (1986) asked children aged 6 and 7 years,
in the USA and in Switzerland respectively, to interpret written numbers,
either by reading them or by showing the number of blocks signified by
the written numbers. The children in their studies had not yet been
taught how to read or write multidigit numbers. They observed that many
of the children treated the digits in two-digit numbers as separate from
each other. For example, when they were shown a card with the number

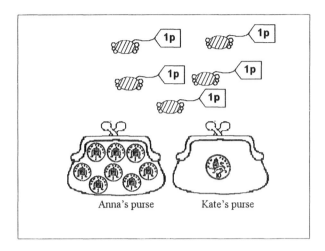

Anna and Kate have money in their purses. They both want to buy some
of the sweets shown in the picture. They want to spend all their money.
How many sweets can Anna buy? How many sweets can Kate buy?
Who has more money?

Figure 4.2 The children are asked to make a correspondence between the money
and the number of sweets that can be bought; the sweets suggest an analogue
representation that can be used to compare one 10p and eight 1p coins.

16 on it and asked to give the researcher blocks that corresponded to the
number written on the card, many children gave the researcher one block
and six blocks. Their investigation suggested that, before instruction, children do not have much insight into how written numbers work.

Perhaps this is not the best way to investigate children's informal
knowledge of written numbers. We know from research on pre-readers
that children are more willing to *write* words at the request of a
researcher before instruction than to try to *read* words. Therefore in our
investigations we (Nunes Carraher, 1982, 1985; Nunes Carraher and
Schliemann, 1983) attempted another route: we asked un-instructed children to *write* numbers. Children who have not been instructed on how
to read and write multidigit numbers not only are willing to write numbers at the request of a researcher but also do so with a system of their
own. Analysing the systems they use can give valuable insight into what
they might know about the conventions before school.

We (Nunes and Bryant, 1996) asked English children aged 5 and 6
years, who had not been taught to write multidigit numbers, to write
some numbers for us. The numbers we asked them to write had one, two,
three or four digits. Among the multidigit numbers, we asked them to

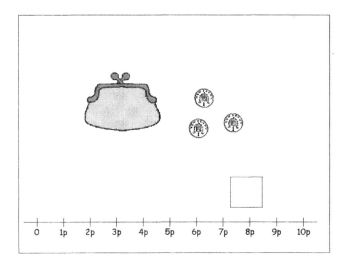

Jo has 5p in her purse. She got more money from her Granny. How
much money does she have now? Write your answer in the box.

Figure 4.3 A hidden addend problem used to cue the children to the use of
analogue representations. The number line is provided as a resource.

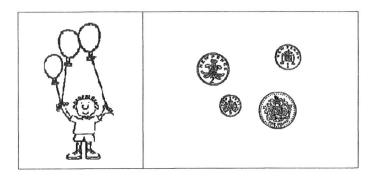

Each balloon costs 2p. Tick the coin that you would use to
pay the exact money for one balloon.

Figure 4.4 A problem used to introduce the idea of paying exact money.

write round numbers, such as 100, 200, 1000, 2000, and numbers where
other digits, different from zero, occupy the different positions.

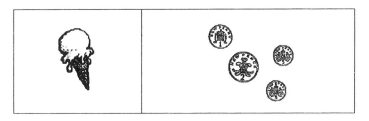

The ice-cream cone costs 7p. Tick the coins you would use
to pay the exact money.

Figure 4.5 An additive composition item using 5p and 1p coins.

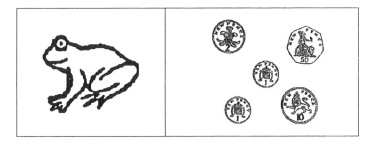

The frog costs 11p. Tick the coins you need to pay the
exact money.

Figure 4.6 An additive composition item using 10p and 1p coins.

The children's performance could be analysed into groups of productions that seemed to be based on a similar system. A few children used a
one-to-one correspondence between words and number. So they used
one digit for one-digit numbers such as 6 and 8. They also used a single
digit for 15 and 60 because these are expressed in one word, but used two
digits for 25 and 47 and also for 'one hundred' and 'two hundred', which
contain two words. This was not a very common production – only 4% of
the children used this system. Children who use this one-to-one correspondence between words and digits often also use non-digits in their
number writing – for example, the pound sign (£) was introduced by a
child between digits to represent the word 'thousand' and a second child
used a sign that looked like the mirror-image of the letter 'e' to represent
the word 'hundred'. The importance of this observation is that it shows
that some children think there is a direct connection between words and

digits – and their production shows very clearly that a direct connection does not work.

A very common system, used by the majority of the children in the age range we investigated (5 and 6 years), is exemplified by Theo's number writing, presented in Figure 4.7. We termed this type of writing *concatenation*, because the children write the numbers in full and as a sequence, without using place value as a convention. They are clearly not matching words to digits on a one-to-one basis. Many children at this age level, like Theo, discover how two-digit numbers are written correctly, even before they are taught how to write numbers in school. Theo correctly wrote 56, his house number, but also 42, 39 and 99, which have no particular significance for him. Looking at their writing of two-digit numbers, we could conclude that they have understood place value. However, with numbers above 100, they tend to use concatenation, except for the well-memorized numbers, such as the calendar year. Note that Theo wrote 2003 with two zeros but used four zeros for 2010. Theo used two zeros for all the numbers in the hundreds and four zeros for all numbers in the thousands, placing the remaining digits after these zeros. The number 5124 is a real challenge – but Theo could not only write it in his system but also read it back. This is a feat not accomplished by the children who use one sign for each word in a number.

Children who have made as much progress as Theo rarely use non-digits in their number writing. This suggests that they have learned at least two things about number writing before instruction: they have learned valid signs – digits – for writing numbers, and they are using the idea of additive composition. The writing of 10005008 for 1508 suggests an implicit knowledge of additive composition. Note that this production does not use a one-to-one correspondence between words and digits: one thousand five hundred and eight contains five number words and eight digits in this production.

It is difficult to say where the children get these ideas from – and it is amazing to know that children in England as well as in Italy (Power and Dal Martelo, 1990), France and Belgium (Seron and Fayol, 1994), Brazil (Nunes Carraher, 1982; Silva, 1993), and Spain (Fuentes, 1999; Fuentes and Tolchinsky, 1999, 2004) come up with the same ideas. The fact that this idea comes up in environments that differ both culturally and linguistically led us to hypothesize that the children are seeking a logical system to support their number writing. They do not expect written numbers to be entirely arbitrary, but related to rules of production. It is possible that they reason that, if counting words have a system, so written numbers should have a system too. So it is quite possible that they are already implicitly using the idea of additive composition but have not learned the place-value conventions yet.

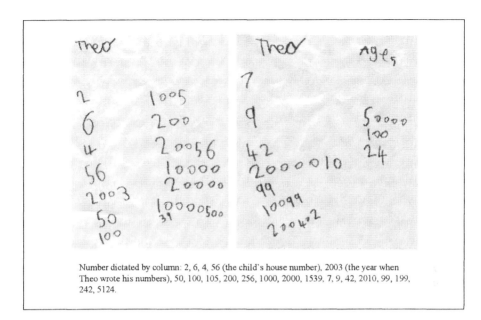

Number dictated by column: 2, 6, 4, 56 (the child's house number), 2003 (the year when Theo wrote his numbers), 50, 100, 105, 200, 256, 1000, 2000, 1539, 7, 9, 42, 2010, 99, 199, 242, 5124.

Figure 4.7 Theo's number writing.

In spite of the children's interest in written numbers and their attempts to crack the code and discover how adults write numbers, the task of mastering the place-value system is not easy. Children continue to make mistakes in writing and reading numbers, and often seem to move backward rather than forward when they are taught a new value. For example, sometimes when children learn about millions, they start making mistakes on thousands, which they appeared to have mastered before (Fuentes and Tolchinsky, 1999, 2004; see also Perret, 1985).

Fuentes and Tolchinsky (1999) carried out a detailed observation of how deaf children, users of Catalan Sign Language (CSL), performed in reading and writing multidigit numbers. CSL, like BSL, has numeral signs for 1 to 10, a sign for zero, and signs for hundred, thousand, million and billion. Also similar to BSL, the number 20 is signed by combining a 2 and a zero, with the zero placed slightly to the right of the 2; 21 is similarly signed with a 2 and a 1, placed to the right of the 2; and so on. So the decades are signed very similarly to how they are written. However, there is no one-to-one match between written numbers and CSL. The number 100 is not signed as 1, zero, zero: there is a sign for hundred. This sign is optional in a number such as 249, which can be signed as a sequence, 2, 4, 9. The number 1000 is not signed by a 1 and three zeros: it is signed as a one plus a specific sign for thousand. The sign for thousand is not optional and must be included when reading a written number: the number 2456 includes four signs, one for each digit, plus the sign for thousand, or six signs in total if the sign for hundred is also used.

Fuentes and Tolchinsky investigated the difficulties in reading and writing numbers faced by deaf children who were users of CSL. They expected that the children would find it easier to write than to read numbers. They reasoned that in order to write, for example, 243, when the number is signed to them without the sign for hundred, the children could simply produce the digits on paper in the same order that these were signed, without necessarily having to understand that the digit 2 represents the number of hundreds and that the digit 4 represents the number of tens. The same system could be used to write numbers in the thousands, if the children learn to ignore the sign for thousand used between the signed digits. In contrast, in order to read the same numbers, they would have to understand where the signs for hundred and for thousand must be placed. Therefore Fuentes and Tolchinsky expected that the children would show greater success in a number writing task than in a number reading task. It should be noted that there is considerable similarity between CSL and BSL in this respect, so it is possible that the same applies to deaf children who use BSL.

Fuentes and Tolchinsky (1999) asked seven children, in the age range 11 to 15, to write and read some numbers. All the children were profoundly deaf from birth and born to hearing parents. Two of the children attended mainstream classes, two were in special classes for deaf pupils, and the other three were in classes that combined activities for the deaf and activities for deaf only and hearing children together. The language policy was bilingual, combining sign and oral language. Four children had Catalan and three had Spanish as their oral language. All children were competent in CSL at the time of testing.

The children were asked to read 60 numbers, which were chosen to exemplify a variety of difficulties in the place-value system. For example, the same digit could appear in the different positions, indicating units, tens, hundreds or thousands. The numbers also included internal zeros (for example, 3005) and round values (1000). The numbers varied in number of digits, from one to six digits.

The reading task was given before the writing task, which included only the numbers that had caused difficulty in the reading task. There was a 3-month interval between the reading and the writing tasks. These two aspects of the design of this study – the use of only a smaller sample of numbers and the longish interval between the two tasks – makes it difficult to reach conclusions about the relative difficulty of the two tasks, which was the aim of the researchers. However, the error analysis that they present is very instructive, and allows for a comparison between hearing and deaf children's ideas about written numbers.

Fuentes and Tolchinsky report two different types of error. One type of error is termed *lexical* error, and consists in using the wrong digit, for example writing (or reading) 784 when the number was 684. The other type of error is termed *syntactic* error, and consists in representing the place value inappropriately. In writing, this essentially means using the wrong number of digits, for example writing 148 or 100048 for 1048. In both cases, the place-value convention was not respected and the wrong number of digits was used. In reading, this could mean, for example, failing to use the sign for thousand when reading 1048, and thus signing 148, which could be interpreted as one hundred and forty-eight. Another example of syntactic error would be to sign one, zero, zero, eight for the number 108. This number can be signed either as one, zero, eight or as one, hundred, eight.

Although all the children were competent in CSL, not all of their responses were signed when they read numbers: one child used oral language only and most children used some oral responses even if they signed many of their reading responses. In the writing task, the teacher always signed the numbers. So their analysis of results separates out signed from oral responses in the reading task.

In summary, their results showed that the children produced more correct than incorrect responses on both tasks, reading and writing. There were some refusals in the reading task (about 8% of the items were refused by children who were using oral language and 2% by children who were using sign) but no refusals in writing. The fact that there were more refusals when the children were attempting to use oral than sign language makes comparisons between the two modalities of language difficult, because it is not clear how to treat a refusal. Should it be treated as error or should these be excluded when calculating the children's mean scores? Fuentes and Tolchinsky carried out both analyses and found that the mean number of correct responses was higher in CSL than in oral language if the refusals were treated as errors, but the difference between performance in the two modalities of language became very small if the refusals were excluded from the total number of responses. It is difficult to interpret the significance of this difference, because the children were not required to carry out the task in one modality: it was their choice to use sign or oral language. So it is not clear why they chose not to sign but to say that they did not know how to read some numbers.

The rate of correct responses was higher in the writing than in the reading task. The rates, ignoring the refusals, were 54% correct for oral reading, 64% for reading through sign, and 83% for writing numbers. Because we do not have comparable figures for hearing children in Spain in the same age range or year of instruction, it is difficult to assess the significance of these percentages, so we do not know whether there is a delay in the deaf children's performance and, if there is, how large the gap between hearing and deaf pupils is.

The most interesting results come from the analysis of errors that Fuentes and Tolchinsky carried out. These results are summarized in Table 4.3.

Table 4.3 Percentage of error type in reading numbers (by language used by the child) and in writing numbers

	Syntactic errors	Lexical errors	Others
Reading task			
Oral language	81	16	3
Sign language	82	17	1
Writing task	67	29	4

The percentages suggest that children find it much easier to identify a written digit with its oral or signed representation than to master the place-value conventions. Both in reading and writing numbers, the percentage of syntactic errors is greater than the percentage of lexical errors. This result is in line with trends described in different sources regarding hearing children's errors in writing numbers. Our own research, described briefly earlier on, showed that less than 10% of the errors made by hearing 5- and 6-year-olds were lexical. So for both hearing and deaf children the most difficult aspect of written numbers is not to learn which written digits represent which oral or signed numbers but to learn the conventions.

In summary, an error analysis of children's production suggests that the task of learning to read and write numbers is not one mostly of memory, but one of understanding the place-value conventions (whether the child is hearing or deaf). Lexical errors, which are a matter of memory, are much less common. They may be more common for deaf than for hearing children, but presently there are no results to indicate this. Syntactic errors, which are violations of the place-value conventions, are the most common type of error – and most likely should be dealt with by trying to lead the children to understand how the conventions work.

This brings us back to the issue of logic. It was argued that the conventions are based on a logic that supports the system. So we now turn to the evidence that examined whether logic really matters.

Does the logic of additive composition really matter?

In this chapter, it has been argued so far that the two concepts assessed on the Shop Task – the concepts of units and additive composition, are crucial for children's understanding of numbers. It was argued that children can only understand that, say, the 4 in 48 represents 40 if they understand the idea of different units and that this is not all: they still need to understand that 48 is composed of 40 + 8 to be able to read and write numbers using our place-value system. How can we know if these concepts are really related to children's ability to read and write numbers?

Our research with hearing children (see Nunes and Bryant, 1996) gave us a first look at the importance of additive composition for children's learning of written numbers. We gave the Shop Task to a group of hearing children in their second year of school (aged about six and a half) and we also assessed their ability to write numbers – a task that the teacher had just started to teach them. The children's performance on the Shop Task allowed us to classify them into two groups: one group who showed little or no understanding of additive composition and a second group who succeeded in most or all of the items. Very few children showed an intermediary performance. We then looked at their ability to write numbers in the hundreds and thousands. The children in the group that did not understand additive composition were able to produce 13% correct responses. In contrast, the children who showed a good understanding of additive composition produced 60% correct responses. This difference was statistically significant. This result is important because the children were all in the same class and were receiving the same teaching in school.

However, our study analysed only the connection between additive composition and reading and writing numbers. Our hypothesis is that this connection has implications that reach much further. Understanding the additive composition of numbers is important for reading and writing numbers, but it is also important for learning mathematics in general, because written numbers become the main form of number representation in the mathematics classroom. So our hypothesis is that the logic of numbers, as assessed on the Shop Task, provides the foundation on which much mathematics learning has to be built during primary school. How can this broader hypothesis be tested?

Chapter 1 introduced the use of correlations to test causal hypotheses in psychology. If the children's success on the Shop Task is an indicator that they have a good understanding of ideas that are crucial to understanding numbers, there should be a strong correlation between their performance on the Shop Task and their success in mathematics tests in general.

Moreno (2000) has recently shown that the Shop Task is significantly correlated with deaf children's performance in a standardized mathematics test, the NFER-Nelson Age Appropriate Tests. The 42 deaf children in her study were classified into three levels of performance on the Shop Task. She assigned them either to a group that showed *no understanding* of additive composition, having received a score of 0 or 1 in the eight items; or to a second group that showed *some understanding* of additive composition, having received a score between 2 and 5; or to a third group that showed *good understanding* of additive composition, having received a score between 6 and 8. She then analysed whether the children's performance on the Shop Task was significantly correlated with their performance on the standardized mathematics assessment. She found a high and significant correlation between the children's performance on the Shop Task and their performance on the standardized assessment ($r = 0.63$; $p < 0.001$).

However, as stressed in Chapter 1, correlations must be interpreted with caution. It is possible that knowledge of additive composition is a cause of good performance in mathematics, because it provides a necessary grounding for the understanding of numbers, but it is also possible that both of these abilities are caused by a third one – for example, the children's intelligence. The more able the children, the more easily they learn about additive composition informally and also the more easily they learn mathematics in school.

Psychologists use a statistical method, called *regression analysis* to separate out the effect that intelligence has on both abilities – knowledge of additive composition and mathematical ability in general – from the relation that they have with each other and which is not part of their connection with intelligence. By subtracting what these three competencies have in common, if there is still something in common between the children's understanding of additive composition and their performance on the standardized mathematics tests, whatever is still common to these two abilities is not due to intelligence. Figure 4.8 illustrates this method graphically.

Moreno (2000) carried out a regression analysis in order to see how much variance in common there is between the additive composition and mathematical achievement when the common variance between the three abilities – intelligence, mathematical achievement and knowledge of additive composition – has been separated out. She also had to control for the children's age in her analysis, because they varied in age and, consequently, education. She found that age and education had 16% of variance in common with the children's performance on the NFER test; their performance on the WISC intelligence test (the Wechsler Intelligence Scale for Children: Wechsler, 1974) had a further 15% of common variance with

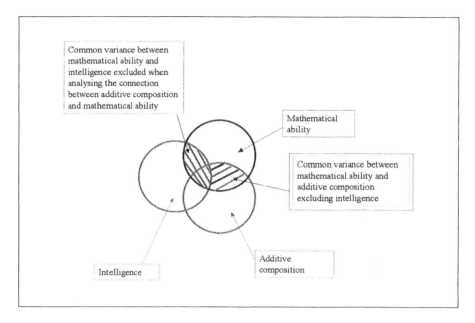

Figure 4.8 A diagram showing common variance between mathematical ability, additive composition, and intelligence.

mathematical ability. After separating out these effects of education and intelligence, the children's performance on the Shop Task still had plenty of common variance with the standardized test: 17% of the variance in the children's scores on the NFER test was still related to their performance in additive composition. This analysis suggests that there is an important connection between the knowledge that deaf children have acquired of additive composition and their performance on a standardized mathematics assessment.

But there is a second danger in correlational analyses, as discussed in Chapter 1. It is possible that children's informal knowledge of additive composition provides a good basis for their understanding of numbers, but the cause–effect relation could go the other way round: perhaps it is children's good understanding of numbers that leads them to understand additive composition. What do psychologists do to solve this dilemma?

Researchers reason that the cause in this case should come before the effect. If it is the children's informal knowledge of additive composition that provides a good grounding for them to learn about numbers, it should be possible to show that this is so by finding that their knowledge of additive composition at an earlier occasion predicts how well they learn mathematics at a later time.

To investigate this, psychologists carry out *longitudinal studies*. In a longitudinal study, we test the children at Time 1 using the assessment that measures what we think is the cause. So, in order to test our hypothesis, the children should be assessed in additive composition at Time 1. Some time later, at Time 2, we test the children using the second assessment, which measures what we think is the consequence – in this case, the children should receive the standardized mathematics assessment. If the children's performance on the Shop Task at Time 1 can help us predict how well they will perform in a mathematics assessment at Time 2, after controlling for what both of these tests have in common with education and intelligence, then we can have some confidence in our hypothesis – that is, we can have confidence in the idea that children's informal understanding of additive composition provides them with a good grounding for learning about numbers.

Moreno (2000), again, was the first researcher to carry out this investigation with deaf children. She gave the children the Shop Task and the intelligence test at Time 1. At Time 2, 4 months later, she gave them the NFER Test. At Time 3, 8 months later, she gave them an assessment of their mathematics age.

Her results can be summarized very simply: at both times, after separating out the variance that mathematical ability had in common with education and intelligence, the children's mathematical ability still had considerable variance in common with the Shop Task at Time 1. For the NFER test given at Time 2, 4 months after the Shop Task, there was 12% common variance between the Shop Task and the mathematics assessment. For the mathematics age test given at Time 3, 8 months after the Shop Task, the common variance was 18%, after excluding the effects of education and intelligence.

These results are considered very strong evidence that children's understanding of additive composition does, in fact, matter for how well they perform later in mathematics tests. They support the idea that children's knowledge of additive composition, which hearing children often acquire informally and before school, provides them with a solid basis for learning about numbers. Therefore these findings suggest that it is important to ensure that deaf children, who may start school without having acquired this informal knowledge, have the opportunity to learn about additive composition quite early in their school life.

In summary, hearing children learn much about additive composition before starting school. Their knowledge may come from a variety of sources, but one of them is their experience with money. One reason that money offers children an opportunity to learn about the concepts of units and additive composition is that different denominations of coins are units of different values, which can be combined to make up a single value.

A second reason is that money represents these units symbolically, rather than in an analogue manner, and therefore it places demands on the children's reasoning that are quite similar to reading and writing numbers. A common method used in school to help children understand additive composition is to represent quantities with the Unifix bricks, which can be put together in tens, forming a long rod, and singles. When representing, for example, 28 with Unifix bricks, the children should use two long rods, with ten bricks in each, and eight singles. This practice is very common in schools and was used in the schools where the children assessed by Moreno were enrolled. So why were there so many deaf 7- and 8-year-olds who, in spite of this teaching, did not succeed on the Shop Task? Our research suggests one reason why the Unifix bricks may not help the children reach the more advanced understanding of additive composition required on the Shop Task. The number representation with Unifix bricks is an analogue representation: each unit is visible and can be counted. It was shown earlier on in this chapter that children who succeed in tasks that use analogue representations can fail in other similar tasks, when symbolic representations are used. Because Unifix bricks do not help the children make the transition from analogue to symbolic representations, they do not support the children's learning to the point that has to be reached for a good basis for learning to read and write numbers to be built.

For many reasons, deaf children often have fewer opportunities to learn about things that happen outside the home – and money seems to be one of them. In Chapter 1 it was already mentioned that deaf children are behind hearing children in their understanding of money concepts (Austin, 1975). So preschool- and schoolteachers should bear in mind that they need to create opportunities for deaf children to explore these concepts. Analogue representation of units larger than one can offer children a good starting point to work on the concept of units. Frydman and Bryant's work with hearing children and our work with deaf children show that analogue representations help children take the first step towards understanding symbolic representations of units larger than one. Both manipulative materials and the number line can be used to start the children along the path of mastering the idea of additive composition of numbers. But it should not be forgotten that analogue representations do not suffice: the children must be able to go beyond them in order to understand numbers. This is why supporting children's performance in situations like the Shop Task, where symbolic representations are used, can have a positive impact on their later learning.

CHAPTER 5

Multiplicative reasoning: connecting multiplication, division and many other mathematical ideas

The aims of this chapter are to analyse what is at the core of multiplicative reasoning, how hearing and deaf children develop these ideas informally outside school, and how schools can promote further development in their multiplicative reasoning. Similarly to previous chapters, it must be recognized from the outset that, although there is some consistency in the analysis of multiplicative reasoning provided by different researchers, there is no theory about this domain of mathematical reasoning that is accepted by all. However, there is probably a larger gap between researchers' views and teaching practices than there is between the different views held by researchers in this domain.

The first discrepancy between educational practice and psychological research has to do with the assumptions about what young children know about multiplication and division. Educational practice and traditional curricula seem to assume that not only young children – at ages 5 or 6 – do not know anything about multiplication and division, but also that they should not or could not be taught anything related to multiplication and division at these early ages. The teaching of multiplication and division is introduced much later, when the children have had considerable experience with addition and subtraction. This contrasts with results from research carried out by child psychologists in different countries, which shows that 5- and 6-year-olds do have some informal knowledge of multiplication and division that could be used as a basis for further learning in school.

The second divergence between psychological research and educational practice relates to the conceptual basis of multiplicative reasoning. Educational practice typically treats multiplication as repeated addition. Researchers in psychology and mathematics education have moved a considerable distance from the idea that multiplication is simply repeated addition. Although different descriptions have been offered of the situations that give meaning to the multiplicative reasoning, there is little doubt that the logic of multiplication involves much more than the idea of repeated addition. As will be argued later in this chapter, multiplicative reasoning involves thinking about relations between variables, and this involves reasoning that is considerably different from thinking about part–whole relations, which characterizes additive reasoning.

The first section of this chapter analyses how children develop an understanding of the logic of relations between variables in informal situations and how their informal knowledge can be used as the starting point for teaching multiplication. Research about deaf children in this domain is scarce. We will present results from our own research (Nunes, 1995), which have not previously been published elsewhere. We know of no other studies that analysed deaf children's informal knowledge of multiplicative reasoning. The second section considers the classification of multiplicative reasoning situations that we have found most useful in the design of our investigations of children's reasoning and of instruction. It would be beyond the purpose of this book to analyse in great detail a classification of multiplicative situations. As with our review of studies on additive reasoning, we would not like to claim that this chapter offers a synthesis of theories and research about multiplicative reasoning. It attempts instead to look with a magnifying lens at children's informal knowledge of multiplicative reasoning and ways in which schools can build on their knowledge to further their mathematical ability. The third section considers ways of representing multiplicative reasoning situations, discussing the importance of appropriate analogue and symbolic representations. The final section presents a teaching experiment where visual representations of multiplicative situations were used to support deaf children's learning. The assessment of this teaching programme is discussed in Chapter 6.

What is at the core of multiplicative reasoning?

It was argued in Chapter 3 that additive reasoning is related to children's actions of joining, separating, and placing in one-to-one correspondence. Joining and separating are connected to addition and subtraction in a very direct way; one-to-one correspondence was identified as the informal knowledge that children use to solve comparison problems. Joining and separating are inverse actions to each other: the action of joining two parts can be cancelled by separating them again, just as the operations of addition and subtraction are inverse operations to each other.

The situation with multiplicative reasoning is slightly more complicated. Multiplicative reasoning, it will be argued, is also related to children's actions: multiplication is related to one-to-many correspondences, and division is related to sharing. So far, things seem as easy as they were with additive reasoning. However, the connection between the actions of setting in correspondence and sharing is less obvious than the connection between joining and separating: setting in correspondence and sharing are not readily seen as actions that can cancel each other out. This makes it considerably more difficult to coordinate the discussion of these two action schemes in one section. Thus this section considers first the issues related to one-to-many correspondences and later to sharing.

One-to-many correspondence and multiplication

Multiplication situations involve the idea that there is a *fixed ratio between two quantities (or variables)*. Think, for example, of typical multiplication problems children are asked to solve in school. (1) Angela bought 3 boxes of eggs; each box had 6 eggs; how many eggs did she buy? In this problem, there is a fixed ratio between the number of boxes and the number of eggs: each box corresponds to 6 eggs. (2) Simeon has just filled 4 stamp books with stamps; each book holds 25 stamps; how many stamps does he have in his collection? In this example, the ratio is: each book corresponds to 25 stamps. These examples are typical of multiplication problems given in school.

It should be stressed that multiplication problems always involve two variables (at least): in the examples above, number of boxes and number of eggs per box; or number of books and number of stamps per book. The logic involved in these problems concerns the relation between variables. This makes multiplicative reasoning problems quite different from additive reasoning problems, where the logic concerns part–whole relations.

Some authors (Brown, 1981; Hart, 1981) distinguish problems where the ratio given is 1 to x, which they call *rate* problems, from those where the value corresponding to a unit is not given, which they term *ratio* problems. This distinction is to some extent important, because problems where the children are told the unit rate do result in a greater percentage of success than those where the unit rate is not given. However, this is not a difference between the logical aspects of the problems, but rather a difference in the calculation moves required for solution. In this discussion we will refer simply to fixed ratio as the core of the logic of multiplication problems and will not make a distinction between rate and ratio.[1]

---

[1]   Some authors consider problems where the question refers to a relation between numbers as a special multiplication situation. For example, Gina has 4 apples and Roger has three times as many; how many apples does Roger have? This problem can be thought of as a ratio problem: for each apple that Gina has, Roger has 3 apples. However, children do not seem to think of such problems as fixed ratio situations. They treat them more like repeated addition: they represent the number of apples that Gina has three times. There is agreement in the literature that these problems should be considered as one-variable problems (Brown, 1981; Vergnaud, 1983) because the situation describes a multiplying factor but not a relation between variables. These problems are usually easy and reveal little about children's understanding of multiplicative situations, so they are not considered in this chapter.

Piaget (1952) suggested that the origin of children's understanding of multiplicative reasoning is in their understanding of correspondences. The connection between the ideas of ratio and correspondence is quite easy to see: in the problems presented above, the ratio 1 to 6 can easily be expressed as 'each box corresponds to 6 eggs'. Piaget's hypothesis is important because it shows how it is possible for children to develop informal knowledge of multiplication: ratio is an abstract idea, perhaps not easily grasped, but correspondences can be acted out. Children can for example set 6 eggs in correspondence with each of three boxes in order to figure out how many eggs Angela, in example (1), bought. This means that it is possible that children develop some informal knowledge of multiplicative situations through the use of correspondence reasoning.

Piaget's investigations (1952) indicate that 5- and 6-year-olds can make logical inferences about sets that are in one-to-many correspondence. He asked the children in his study to set two flowers in correspondence with each vase, by first creating a set of yellow flowers in correspondence with the vases and then creating a set of red flowers in correspondence with the same vases. He then put the flowers aside and asked the children to take from a box the exact number of straws that were needed to place one flower into each straw. The children could not see the flowers – only the vases. Piaget reasoned that, if the children understood correspondence reasoning, they would place two straws in correspondence with each vase. In this way, they would have the same number of straws as flowers. This type of reasoning is formally represented by the expression 'If $A = 2B$ and $C = 2B$, then $A = C$', and is known as a transitive inference. The problem set by Piaget requires the children to use their understanding of correspondence to make judgements about quantities. He observed that the majority of the 5- and 6-year-olds did put two straws in front of each vase and obtain the right number of straws. Thus, Piaget argued, they understood that if the number of flowers was equal to two times the number of vases, and the number of straws was also equal to two times the number of vases, the number of flowers and straws would necessarily be the same. The results of Piaget's study are quite clear. They show that children do have some informal knowledge of multiplicative reasoning – in particular, of the role of ratios in determining set sizes – before they are taught about multiplication in school.

Kornilaki (1999) investigated further hearing children's understanding of multiplicative reasoning before they had received instruction on multiplication in school. She worked with 5-, 6- and 7-year-olds and asked them to make a different type of judgement, which involved deciding whether two sets were equal or not. She showed the children a picture of two large houses, where some rabbits were going to live. The rabbits were transported into the houses in little hutches, which were also presented to the

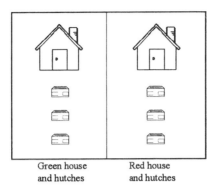

Green house   Red house
and hutches   and hutches

Same number of hutches, different ratios: Each green hutch carries 2
rabbits; they go into the green house. Each red hutch carries 3 rabbits;
they go into the red house. Are there more rabbits in the green house, in
the red house, or is the number of rabbits the same in the two houses?

Figure 5.1 A relational problem about different ratios; from Kornilaki (1999).

children through pictures. The rabbits that would live in the green house
were carried in green hutches and those that would live in the red house
were carried in red hutches. She set the green and red hutches in correspondence in front of the houses, as in Figure 5.1.

Kornilaki worked with four types of situations that required the children to consider the rabbit-to-hutch ratio. The first two types of problem
she termed *relational problems*, because the children did not have to
know how many rabbits would live in the houses in order to answer the
question. In these problems, either the number of hutches was the same
and the ratio of rabbits-to-hutch varied (as in the example presented in
Figure 5.1), or the number of hutches was different and the number of
rabbits inside the hutches of the different colours was the same. The children's level of success in these problems was quite high: 95% of the
5-year-olds and all of the 6- and 7-year-olds solved the problems correctly. Thus they realized that, for example, 3×2 and 3×3 are different, and
that 3×3 is more than 3×2, without having to calculate the number of
rabbits. It did not matter whether the number of hutches was the same
and the ratio different, or the number of hutches was different and the
ratio the same. Both problem types were easy for these young children.

Kornilaki also presented the children with two other problem types,
where both the number of hutches and the rabbit-to-hutch ratio differed. In
one of these problems, the children would not have to calculate the number of rabbits going into the house *if they understood the commutativity
of multiplication*. For example, there were 4 hutches with 2 rabbits in each
in one set and 2 hutches with 4 rabbits in each in the other set. In the sec-

ond problem type, the children would have to calculate the number of rab-bits in each set in order to make the comparison; for example, there were 2 hutches with 5 rabbits in each in one set and 3 hutches with 4 rabbits in each in the other set. Kornilaki observed that, although 5-year-olds had no difficulty with the relational problems, they found these two problem types rather difficult. Only about 16% of the 5-year-olds solved these problems correctly. There was no significant difference in the percentage of correct responses between the problem where commutativity could be used and the problem in which it could not be used. This suggests that the children were not thinking in terms of commutativity but were trying to figure out the number of rabbits living in the hutches in both types of problems. The 6- and 7-year-olds were more successful: 60% of the 6-year-olds and 86% of the 7-year-olds provided correct responses. Like the 5-year-olds, they were not helped by the possibility of using the commutativity of multiplication to solve one of the problem types, and the percentages of correct responses did not vary across these two types of problems.

In our study of deaf children's mathematical reasoning, we presented 82 children with the two relational problems developed by Kornilaki. In order to simplify the situation, we used cut-out drawings of lorries and warehouses, where the lorries were going to unload bags of sugar. As in the Kornilaki study, the green and blue lorries were going to unload the bags they carried into warehouses of the same colour, green and blue, respectively. We asked the children to imagine that there were bags of sugar inside the lorries and indicated the number of bags inside each one using their preferred language (English, SSE or BSL); for the children who were being educated orally, we also indicated with fingers the number of bags. We then acted out the unloading process by moving the lorries over the warehouses and turning them upside down. Finally we asked the chil-dren whether there would be the same number of bags of sugar inside the warehouses or whether the number was different; if their answer was 'dif-ferent', we asked them to indicate which warehouse had more bags inside.

The children were in Years 2, 3, 4 and 5 at school. Their mean ages, respectively, were 6 years 9 months, 8 years 3 months, 9 years, and 9 years 10 months. Just as with the hearing children, the deaf children were equally successful with both types of relational problems. It did not mat-ter whether the number of lorries was the same and the bags-to-lorry ratio varied, or whether the number of lorries was different and the bags-to-lorry ratio was the same. The percentages of correct responses for each year group in school were: 80% correct for Year 2 children, 75% correct for Year 3, 100% correct for Year 4 and 91% correct for Year 5. In spite of some fluctuation in the percentages of correct responses across the year groups, these results are very positive. The performance of the 6- and 7-year-old deaf children shows that they have developed some informal knowledge of multiplication before they are taught about multiplication in school. There is a gap between hearing and deaf children – all the 6-year-old hearing children answered these problems correctly and 80% of the deaf children in this age group gave correct answers – but the gap does not seem very wide.

The next question we considered was whether the deaf children can use their correspondence reasoning as well as hearing children to solve problems where they are asked to give a numerical answer. Kornilaki used different problem types to assess the children's ability to figure out a numerical answer. Because our investigation included so many questions and we did not want to burden the children with even more problems, we asked the children to provide a numerical answer to the same problems above: we asked them how many bags of sugar would be in each of the warehouses. We ensured that they still remembered how many bags were inside the lorries and left the lorries in full sight. Hearing children's informal solution to these computational problems involve counting in a way that preserves the correspondence between the two variables in the problem. For example, when the children in Kornilaki's study had to figure out how many rabbits there were altogether when 4 hutches had 3 rabbits in each, they would point three times to each hutch as they counted: one, two, three – four, five, six – seven, eight, nine – ten, eleven, twelve. We saw in Chapter 2 that deaf children show a delay in counting in comparison to hearing children. So we expected that there would be a delay in their ability to solve these problems through counting. The question is how severe this delay might be. We certainly expected it to be much more marked than the small delay observed on the relational problems.

The percentages of correct responses observed among the deaf children by year group in school were: 31% for Year 2, 42% for Year 3, 26% for Year 4, and 41% for Year 5. These results confirm that the need to combine their knowledge of correspondences with counting made this problem more difficult for the deaf children. Although a considerable number of the deaf children showed a good understanding of correspondences in the relational problems, a much smaller number was able to use this knowledge to indicate how many bags of sugar were in the warehouses. It is noteworthy that the amount of progress made with schooling was modest. A statistical analysis using chi-square showed that there was no association between level of schooling and success in this problem. These results suggest that perhaps schools are not currently helping the deaf children use their informal knowledge to solve multiplication problems. It is quite possible that appropriately targeted instruction could help deaf children use their informal knowledge of correspondence in connection with counting and that their performance on these tasks would improve considerably.

Multiplication problems with a missing factor

So far we have discussed only problems where the correspondence scheme can be applied directly in order to find a solution: there are 4 hutches; 3 rabbits in each; how many rabbits altogether? If the children are given manipulative materials, such as cut-out figures and blocks, they can set three blocks in correspondence with the hutches and find the right answer.

Kornilaki (1999) analysed what happens when hearing children attempt to solve problems where one of the factors in the multiplication situation is missing. She termed the latter problems *inverse*, by analogy with direct and inverse additive situations (see Chapter 3). She reasoned that, if it is true that young children solve multiplicative situation problems using correspondence reasoning, it should be possible to make predictions about the level of difficulty of the different inverse problems by analysing how easily the children can solve these problems using correspondences. If her predictions are correct, this will make us more confident that children do use correspondences when thinking about multiplicative situations.

Here are three examples of the problems she used. Her *direct* correspondence problem was: 'I bought 3 boxes of chocolate. Each box had 4 chocolates in it. How many chocolates do I have?' The formal representation for this problem is: $3 \times 4 = ?$

Kornilaki designed two *inverse*, missing-factor problems. In the first type of inverse problem, the children were told the ratio between the quantities: 'I had a party. Each child that came brought me 3 flowers. I got 15 flowers. How many children came?' The formal representation for this problem is $? \times 3 = 15$. In the second type, the children are not told the ratio between the quantities: 'I had a party. Three children came. Each child brought me the same number of flowers. I got 15 flowers. How many flowers did each child bring?' The formal representation for this problem is $3 \times ? = 15$.

In all three problems the situations described involve a fixed ratio between two variables. However, Kornilaki did not expect that it would be equally easy for children to apply their informal knowledge of multiplication to the three types of problem. In the direct problems the connection between correspondence reasoning and the path to solution is simple. The situation can be acted out (or modelled) with objects; no extra reasoning steps are required. All the child has to do to solve a direct multiplication problem is to create representations for each of the variables; for example, the child can use blocks to represent the boxes of chocolates and count the chocolates by pointing four times to each box. If the child is given manipulative materials, such as cut-out figures of boxes and chocolates, the child can set the objects in correspondence.

If the children try to use their knowledge of correspondences to solve the inverse problems, they will face different levels of difficulty depending on which factor is missing. If they know the ratio – 'each child that came brought me three flowers' – they can create groups of 3 flowers until they reach 15 flowers altogether: the number of groups corresponds to the number of children who came to the party. The use of correspondence reasoning certainly must be adapted to solve this problem, but the adaptation is not complicated. It is still possible to use correspondence reasoning and solve the problem. In the second type of inverse problem, where the children are not told the ratio, the use of a correspondence solution is not so simple: 'Three children came to the party, I got 15 flowers' does not provide the children with sufficient information to set up correspondences in a way that will solve the problem.

Kornilaki's analysis leads to the prediction that the children's performance should be significantly worse in the second type of inverse problem than in the first because it is more difficult to use the correspondence reasoning in order to find the answer. Table 5.1 presents a summary of her results with hearing children.

Table 5.1 Percentage of children who succeeded in the different types of correspondence problems, by age level

Age level	Direct problem	Inverse type 1	Inverse type 2
5 years	37	37	10
6 years	70	67	30
7 years	87	87	57
8 years	100	97	80
Total	**73**	**72**	**44**

It is clear that the children's performance in the two problems that can be solved through correspondences – direct and inverse type 1 – is very similar. The percentage of success in these two types of problems was considerably better than in the inverse problem type 2, where the correspondence reasoning cannot be applied with ease. Tests for the significance of the difference between two dependent proportions showed that the inverse problem type 2 was significantly more difficult than the type 1 problem at all age levels.

This study brings support to the analysis proposed here: that children develop informal knowledge of multiplication situations on the basis of their correspondence reasoning. Unfortunately, no similar work exists with deaf children so it is not possible to confirm these trends with them. However, the results described earlier on show that deaf children do develop some informal knowledge of correspondences and can use this knowledge to solve direct problems. It is necessary to carry out further research with deaf children, though, to analyse whether they show a greater delay in inverse than in direct multiplication problems in comparison to hearing children.

Sharing and division

Division situations are easily connected with children's actions when sharing. Even young children, aged 5 years, can divide sets into equal parts by sharing, using a one-for-you and one-for-me distribution. The action of sharing seems quite different from the action of putting things into correspondence, but it should be noted that both of these actions involve the idea of fixed ratio between two variables. For example, consider the division problem: I have 12 sweets to distribute equally to 6 children; how many sweets will each one get? In a fair sharing situation, you can go around and give one sweet to each child, then go around a second time and give a second sweet to each child; the end result of sharing should be a fixed ratio between children and sweets – to each child correspond two sweets. So the idea of fixed ratio is essential in both multiplication and division situations. In multiplicative situations we usually start out by saying what the ratio between the quantities is, whereas in division situations, sharing results in a fixed ratio. But the actions used to represent these multiplication and division situations are quite different: setting quantities in correspondence and sharing do not have an obvious connection to each other.

We saw in the preceding section that both hearing and deaf children can compare two sets that have a fixed ratio to a third set. For example, they know that the total number of bags in a set with a three-to-one ratio to the number of lorries is bigger than a set with a two-to-one ratio to the same number of lorries.

In this section we examine whether children can compare sets using information from sharing situations. A division situation involves three quantities (or variables): the number of objects to be shared, the number of recipients, and the number of objects received by each one. When the number of objects to be shared increases and the number of recipients is the same, each recipient gets more. For example, if the sweets in a bag are to be shared amongst four children, the more sweets in the bag, the more each child will get. This relation – the more sweets, the more each one gets – is termed a *direct relation*. Now, if the number of sweets in the bag is the same, the more children receiving sweets, the fewer each one gets. This relation between the number of recipients and the size of the share – the more children receiving sweets, the fewer they each get – is termed an *inverse relation*.

Investigations with hearing children (Correa, 1994) show that not all children who can share sweets fairly understand that there is a *direct* relation between the number of sweets to be shared and the number that each recipient gets when the number of recipients does not change. Correa asked children to make judgements about the relative sizes of two sets. The problems she presented to the children were of the following form: there are two parties; at one party, there are 12 sweets to be shared among 6 grey rabbits; at the other party, there are 12 sweets to be shared among 6 brown rabbits. She then put two groups of rabbits in different corners of the table, to show the rabbits at the two parties, and asked the children the following. Imagine we give all the 12 sweets out to the 6 grey rabbits in this party and we then give all the other 12 sweets to the 6 brown rabbits in this other party; when this rabbit goes home (showing a grey rabbit from party 1) will he have the same number of sweets as this rabbit (showing a brown rabbit from party 2)?

We used a slightly different version of this problem with deaf children. In our task, the problem presentation was the same as that used by Correa but there were 6 rabbits and 12 sweets at one party and 6 rabbits and 18 sweets at the second party. So the correct answer in Correa's problem was that the two rabbits had the same number of sweets, and in our problem the correct answer was that the two rabbits had a different number of sweets; the one who went to the second party had more sweets. In spite of this difference, we believe that the problems are comparable because they investigate the relation between the corresponding quantities in the sharing situation. The percentages of correct responses observed by Correa for hearing children and in our study with deaf children are presented in Table 5.2. Note that the youngest deaf children in our study are older than the oldest hearing children in Correa's study.

Table 5.2 Percentage of correct responses to a direct relations problem in a division situation, by hearing status and age level

Age	Percentage correct
Hearing children (n − 66)	
5 years	71
6 years	88
7 years	98
Deaf children (n = 63)	
8 years	55
9 years	85
10 years	79

Two features of these results are noteworthy. First, neither hearing nor deaf children performed at ceiling in this task. The relation between the variables in this sharing task is direct – the more sweets there are at the party, the more the rabbits will receive. This was also the case in the multiplication problems discussed earlier on: the more bags of sugar there are in the lorries, the more sugar there will be in the warehouse. In spite of this similarity between the tasks, the direct relations problem about sharing was more difficult both for deaf and for hearing children than the direct relations problem about correspondences. Thus although children have informal knowledge about both multiplication and division situations, both hearing and deaf children find it easier to think about relations between the variables in multiplication than in division problems.

Second, the results show a considerable gap between the hearing and the deaf children's performances. Hearing children's performance is at ceiling at age 7 whereas only about half of the deaf 8-year-olds provided the correct response. Thus it is possible that deaf children could benefit from systematic teaching, enabling them to improve their ability to use their informal knowledge of sharing in order to reason about relations in division situations.

Our next research question was: How do children perform in sharing situations when they have to consider *inverse* relations? Correa, Nunes and Bryant (1998) investigated hearing children's understanding of the inverse relations between variables in a division situation. We designed two different types of problems involving sharing.

In one type, known in the literature as *partitive division*, the children were told the number of sweets and the number of recipients, and asked to think about the size of the share they receive. Our problems were relational problems: we did not ask the children to calculate the number of sweets but to compare the size of the share across two groups of recipients. For example, we told the children that we were organizing two parties, one for the grey rabbits and one for the brown rabbits. We then showed them different numbers of rabbits – for example, 3 grey and 4 brown rabbits. The two groups of rabbits were then placed in separate groups at different corners of the tables. We told the children that we had 12 sweets to share among the grey rabbits and 12 sweets to share among the brown rabbits. The rabbits had little baskets on their backs, where we put the sweets that they received. So we shared the sweets without the children seeing how many sweets we were placing into the baskets. Finally we took one grey and one brown rabbit and asked the children whether they had received the same number of sweets. If the children understood that the more recipients, the fewer each one gets, they would be able to provide the correct answer even if they could not tell how many sweets each rabbit had received.

In the second type of problem, known as a *quotitive division* problem, the situation was the same: there were two parties, and rabbits of different colours were going to the parties. The number of sweets to be shared at the parties was the same. However, the question was different. For example, we told the children that we had 12 sweets to share among the grey rabbits and 12 sweets to share among the brown rabbits. We were going to prepare little plates with the same number of sweets on each plate. For the grey rabbits' party, the plates would have 3 sweets. For the brown rabbits' party, the plates would have 4 sweets. We would use up the sweets and invite as many rabbits as we could, but we could not invite any more rabbits when the sweets were finished. The children were asked to tell us whether we would be able to invite the same number of rabbits to both parties or not. If the children understood that the more sweets you give to each rabbit, the fewer rabbits you can invite, they should be able to tell that we would have to invite fewer rabbits to the brown rabbits' party.

The children in this study were in one of three age levels: 5 years (mean age 5 years 4 months), 6 years (mean age 6 years 3 months) and 7 years (mean age 7 years 3 months). The children answered three problems of each of the two types, using different numbers of sweets and different numbers of recipients (in partitive problems) or share sizes (in quotitive problems). The results are presented in Table 5.3 as percentages of correct responses.

We also gave these problems to 63 deaf schoolchildren in Years 3 to 5. The deaf children answered only one problem of each type because these problems were part of a larger investigation and asking too many questions might have made the problem-solving sessions too long. Their percentages of correct responses for each age level are presented in Table 5.3.

Table 5.3 Percentage of correct responses to the different types of division problems by hearing status and age level

Age	Partitive division	Quotitive division
Hearing children (n = 66)		
5 years	56	30
6 years	65	46
7 years	87	42
Deaf children (n = 63)		
8 years	37	0
9 years	70	25
10 years	63	33

The first feature of the results presented in Table 5.3 that strikes us is that the percentages of correct responses at all age levels are lower than those presented in Table 5.2. For both hearing and deaf children, understanding the direct relation between the number of sweets to be shared and the number of sweets each rabbit receives is much easier than understanding the inverse relation between the number of recipients and the size of the share. Thus although the problems are about relations and about the same type of sharing situations, the difference between direct and inverse relations is an important factor that influences children's level of success.

The second feature of Table 5.3 is that there is a severe delay in deaf children's informal reasoning about division situations, particularly in quotitive problems. From this comparison, however, it is not clear whether their difficulty is due to less experience with the activity of sharing or to less experience in thinking about inverse relations. If they have less experience with the actions involved in sharing, they would find it difficult to carry out these actions in partitive and quotitive situations even when directly instructed to do so. If they do have the informal knowledge of division in action but have not had the experience of reflecting upon what these actions mean for the quantities in the situation, they will show a significant gap between their level of success in sharing and their level of success in the relational problems presented above.

In order to find out whether the deaf children's delay could be explained by a difficulty with sharing itself, we asked all the deaf children in our study to carry out a sharing task, once in a partitive and once in a quotitive division situation. In both problems, the situation was the same as those described earlier on. For the partitive sharing problem, we placed 6 toy rabbits on the tables, gave the children 24 blocks, which were pretend sweets that would be distributed at a party, and asked them to share the sweets and say how many each rabbit received. The percentages of correct responses for each year group in school were: 81% for children in Year 2; 90% for children in Year 3; 100% for children in Year 4; and 86% for children in Year 5. The quotitive problem was presented to the children by piling up some toy rabbits in a corner of the table and saying that we were going to organize a party and distribute sweets to each rabbit that we invited. The children were given 20 blocks to be used as pretend sweets and were told that each rabbit that came to the party would receive 4 sweets. They were then asked how many rabbits could be invited. It must be noted that the use of sharing in this problem involves extra steps in comparison to the partitive situation: the children have to make groups of 4 sweets and realize that, for each group, there is a rabbit that can come to the party. The percentages of correct responses for each year group in school were: 62% for children in Year 2; 79% for children in Year 3; 90% for children in Year 4; and 88% for children in Year 5.

These results suggest that deaf children have experience with sharing and can carry out correct sharing actions when directly asked to do so. In the partitive situation, the children's performance was close to or at ceiling (that is, close to the maximum possible level of correct responding). Even in the quotitive situation, where the solution is not directly obtained by the distribution, more than half of the children in Year 2 (6 years 9 months) responded correctly. The percentage of children who successfully shared the sweets and answered the partitive and quotitive questions is significantly higher than the percentage of the children who answered the relational problems correctly. Note, for example, that 79% of the children in Year 3 solved the quotitive distribution problem, but none of them could tell that it was possible to invite more rabbits to a party where each rabbit was going to receive 3 sweets than to a party where each rabbit was going to receive 4 sweets. This suggests that their delay in the relational problems is not due to lack of experience with sharing. It also suggests that teaching that leads them to think more about relations in division situations should be very effective in improving their reasoning about division, because they will be able to draw upon their experience of sharing.

A final word about these results: the children were more successful in sharing the sweets and answering the division questions 'How many sweets does each rabbit get?' or 'How many rabbits can we invite?' than they were in answering the equivalent computation multiplication problems. However, it is important to remember that it is not possible to make a direct comparison between the two situations. In the multiplication problems, we did not give the children analogue representations for the bags of sugar that were inside the lorries: the children had cut-out pictures of lorries in front of them but no objects with which to represent the bags of sugar. In the division problems, the children had analogue representations of the rabbits and the sweets. We saw earlier on, in Chapter 3, that children find it easier to implement informal solutions when problems are presented with analogue representations. Thus the representations used in the sharing situations could have made these problems easier for the children. Thus we cannot conclude that deaf children find division problems easier than multiplication problems.

To summarize: the origin of children's understanding of multiplication and division problems is based on their actions of sharing and setting things into one-to-many correspondence. Putting two quantities in one-to-many correspondence enables children to find a concrete way of thinking about the abstract idea of ratio, which is essential to all multiplicative reasoning problems. Sharing situations also involve the idea of ratio: a fair distribution in a sharing situation must end with a fixed ratio between recipients and the objects shared. These actions are very different from each other and it is not easy for children to think of them as inverses of each other. Both hearing and deaf children develop informal knowledge of multiplicative reasoning – including direct and inverse relations – independently of the teaching they receive in school. There is only a small gap between hearing and deaf children's use of correspondence reasoning to solve relational problems, but there is a severe gap between the two groups when the problems are set in a sharing situation. However, because deaf children are able both to set objects into correspondence when actually carrying out the actions and to share both in partitive and in quotitive situations, it is quite possible that appropriately designed teaching that builds on their informal knowledge can have a significant impact on their performance on these tasks – and, more generally, on their understanding of multiplicative reasoning.

Before we turn to the teaching experiment we carried out, we consider briefly the types of situations that involve multiplicative reasoning.

A classification of multiplicative reasoning tasks

Different classifications of multiplicative reasoning situations have been proposed in the literature (for reviews, see Greer, 1992, 1994; see also: Fischbein, Deri, Nello and Marino, 1985; Harel and Confrey, 1994; Nesher, 1988; Schwartz, 1988). There is no need to review all these classifications here. Four problem types received special consideration in our investigations with deaf children and design of instruction. These are closely related to the action schemes that have been discussed in the preceding section.

Two quite different types of multiplicative reasoning situations that are connected to the scheme of one-to-many correspondence have been identified by several authors (e.g. Brown, 1981; Vergnaud, 1983, 1988) under different names. Vergnaud's terminology is used here. The first type he refers to as *isomorphism of measures*. Vergnaud used this term, familiar to many in mathematics but less familiar to primary school teachers, to refer to all problems where there is one and only one value in one variable (dimension, measure) that corresponds to each value in another variable (dimension, measure). In a simpler form, isomorphism-of-measures problems are those where there is a one-to-many correspondence between two quantities. These are the situations that were discussed when the basis of children's reasoning about multiplication was presented. As indicated earlier on, correspondence problems can be direct or inverse. Vergnaud represents correspondence problems by means of a table (Table 5.4).

Vergnaud's schematic representation of these problems is useful in the description of multiplication problems because it stresses that there are

Table 5.4 A schematic representation of isomorphism-of-measures situations (adapted from Vergnaud, 1983) to show the connection with problems presented earlier on

Measure 1 (variable, quantity, dimension)	Measure 2 (variable, quantity, dimension)
1 (box; book of stamps)	a (number of eggs in the box; number of stamps in the book)
b (a number of boxes; a number of books)	x (the corresponding number of eggs in the boxes; the corresponding number of stamps in the books)

always two variables in multiplication problems, and to each value in one variable corresponds a value in the other variable. It is also useful because it suggests a form of symbolic representation that can be used to help children think about multiplicative situations – tables. When correspondences between the variables are represented in tables, children can think about a multiplication problem in two different ways. They can be asked: what is the ratio that connects the two variables? This will lead them to realize that the ratio is always the same at any point in the table. They can also be asked: When you double the value in one variable, what must you do to the value of the other variable so that the ratio remains the same? Children will then realize that the value in the other variable must also be doubled.

Previous work has shown that both students and adults find it easy to understand that doubling, tripling, or halving the value of one variable requires that the same is done to the other variable for the ratio to remain the same. Hart (1984), for example, showed that if you give pupils a recipe for onion soup and say that this recipe is for 4 people, and then ask them to figure out how much of the ingredients they needed for 8 people, pupils' preferred path to solution is to double the amount. If they are asked how much for 6 people, their preferred strategy is to halve the amounts and add this to the amount required for 4 people. Our own work with Brazilian students and adults with little schooling showed similar results (Nunes, Schliemann and Carraher, 1993).

This path to solution can seem quite obvious for children in some circumstances but not in others. For example, if you buy twice as many marbles today as you did yesterday, it seems obvious that you will have to pay twice as much money. However, much research has shown that there are problems where this does not seem obvious to hearing children.

Inhelder and Piaget (1958) showed that children tend to think additively, rather than in this multiplicative way, when they are asked to solve some types of problems where the notion of a fixed ratio between two variables is not so clear intuitively. For example, they told the young people in their study that eels have to be fed amounts of food that relate to the length of the eel. They then told the children: An eel that is 9 cm long must be fed 12 pellets of food; how much do you have to feed an eel that is 12 cm long? Many children thought that if the eel is 3 cm longer, then it should receive 3 more pellets of food. The reason for children's choice of an additive solution in a problem like this is not clear. A possible explanation could be as follows: the idea that a fixed amount of food corresponds to each centimetre in the eels does not seem to make the same sense as each marble costing a fixed amount of money. So the correspondence reasoning would not be applied intuitively in the solution to this problem.

To quote another example: Hart (1984) and Hoyles and Noss (1992; Noss and Hoyles, 1996) showed that many young pupils think additively when asked to enlarge a rectangle in a way that keeps it looking the same. For example, given a rectangle with 4 cm as the measure of the base and 3 cm for the height, the pupils may be asked what the height should be if the base is now 8 cm. In this situation, many children think additively: instead of thinking that a rectangle with a base equal to 4 cm was doubled in length when the base was increased to 8 cm, they think that the difference between the small and the large rectangle is 4 cm, and propose to add 4 cm to the height in order to keep the rectangle looking the same. This solution, however, does not work, because the proportions between the base and the height will be changed. It is possible, again, that the idea of a fixed ratio between each centimetre in the base and a certain measure of the height does not make sense intuitively.

Thus, although isomorphism of measures is the model that describes these latter two examples, there is no direct connection between these situations and the idea of correspondences between the values. This analysis suggests that, even when children understand and use one-to-many correspondence well, there is a need to expand the children's informal knowledge so that it can be seen as relevant to a variety of contents that fit the isomorphism-of-measures model. Much discussion of the difficulty of multiplicative reasoning problems in the literature centres on the content of the problems. A detailed analysis of this issue is not possible here. Suffice it to say that, though the difficulty of contents is more significant in multiplicative reasoning than in additive reasoning problems, this does not place the problems into a different class of situations.

There is, however, a different class of multiplicative reasoning situations that can be distinguished from isomorphism-of-measures problems. This class of situations is termed by Vergnaud (1983, 1988) *product of measures* (and by Brown (1981) *Cartesian problems*). The main difference between isomorphism- and product-of-measures situations is the way in which the variables are related. In isomorphism-of-measures situations, there are *two variables related by correspondence*: to each value in one variable corresponds a value in the other variable. In product-of-measures situations, there are *two variables that are not related to each other and a third one, which is the result of combining the first two variables*. A typical example is: Sandy has 3 different coloured T-shirts and 4 different coloured skirts. If she wears each of the T-shirts with each of the skirts, changing them around, how many different outfits can she wear? The two variables – T-shirts and skirts – are not related to each other; the third variable, outfits, is a product of combining each value in one variable with each one in the other variable. If you take just the first T-shirt and combine it with each skirt, you can make 4 different outfits. The same happens with the second and the third T-shirts. By analysing the problem in this way, the connection between correspondence reasoning and product-of-measures problems becomes clear: to each T-shirt correspond as many outfits as there are skirts. This shows why product-of-measures problems are an example of multiplicative reasoning situations. It also shows why these situations seem more difficult, because the third variable, number of outfits, has to be created by the combination of the first two.

Much research shows that product-of-measures problems are more difficult for children than isomorphism-of-measures problems are. Brown (1981) asked a large sample of hearing 12-year-olds to indicate the correct operation for solving two problems: one that involved an isomorphism-of-measures problem and the second involving a product-of-measures problem. She observed that 87% of the children gave correct answers to the isomorphism-of-measures problem whereas 62% gave the correct answer to the product-of-measures problem. We (Nunes and Bryant, 1996) observed an even larger difference between success rates in isomorphism- and product-of-measures problems among hearing 8- and 9-year-olds. The isomorphism-of-measures problem was: In each pack of yoghurt come 4 yoghurt cups; how many cups will you have if you buy 6 packs? The product-of-measures problem was the one involving outfits, this time with T-shirts and pairs of shorts. The children had materials at their disposal – cut-out figures of yoghurts and T-shirts and pairs of shorts – that they could use to help them solve the problems. The vast majority of the children (75% of the 8- and almost all the 9-year-olds) gave correct responses to the isomorphism-of-measures problem. In contrast, only about 25% of the 8- and 50% of the 9-year-olds gave correct responses to the product-of-measures problems.

Our observations of the children's correct solutions suggested that the correct solution was found when the children had the idea of setting each

T-shirt in correspondence with each skirt, finding out the number of outfits for each T-shirt, and then reasoning that the same one-to-many
correspondence would apply to the other T-shirts and skirts. Below is a
dialogue that exemplifies this type of solution.

Interviewer (I):	Now, this girl had 6 pairs of shorts of different colours, you see? Blue, green, brown, yellow, black and red. She also had T-shirts of different colours: blue, green, black and white. By changing around which T-shirt she put on with the different shorts, she could have different outfits, couldn't she? For example, one day she could be all dressed in blue, the next day she could still have the blue shorts on but have the white T-shirt. That would be a different outfit, wouldn't it?
Sarah (S):	Yes.
I:	And if she changed them all around, had all the shorts on with the different T-shirts, how many different ways would she look? How many different outfits?
S:	(Moves all the shorts and puts them next to the blue T-shirt) Six.
I:	(Mistaking the child's comment for the final answer) How do you know ...
S:	With the blue T-shirt.
I:	And with all of them?
S:	Twenty-four.
I:	And how do you know it is twenty-four?
S:	Six times four. (From Nunes and Bryant, 1996: 165–6.)

This dialogue exemplifies the approach used by the successful children to
solve this problem: by combining each T-shirt with one pair of shorts, the
child established that each T-shirt could be used for 6 different outfits
and, so, 4 T-shirts would provide 24 outfits. The analysis of children's
strategies in this study suggested to us a path for teaching children how
to solve product-of-measures problems, which was then used in the intervention study with deaf pupils. This is described in the last section of this
chapter.

The example given so far of product-of-measures problems could make
it seem that product-of-measures situations are trivial. However, it is only
an example of a situation that children can understand and that can be
represented with concrete materials. Product-of-measures problems are

very important for understanding a variety of mathematical and scientific concepts. Area, for example, is typically treated as a product-of-measures problem, because we obtain a third measure – square metres – by multiplying two simple ones, the measures of the base and of the height, neither of which is in square metres. Volume involves a product of three measures, producing cubic metres. These are simple examples of *product of measures*; for further discussion, see Nunes and Bryant (1996).

Our study with 63 deaf children in school year groups 3 to 5 (age range 8 to 10 years) showed a similar discrepancy between the percentage of correct responses to isomorphism and product of measures problems. As indicated earlier on in this chapter, the percentage of correct responses varied between 26% and 42% for the children in this age range in isomorphism-of-measures problems. The product-of-measures problem we asked the deaf children to solve was the same one about outfits we had presented to hearing children. Only one 8-year-old (out of 20) and two 10-year-olds (out of 24) responded correctly to the product-of-measures problem.

The children's problem-solving strategies showed that their errors were very similar to those observed with hearing children. At first it was difficult to explain the idea of combining the T-shirts and shorts in different ways to make different outfits. So some children initially answered that it was only possible to make 4 outfits because there were only 4 T-shirts. Once this idea was explained by saying that on one day Sandy used one combination and on a different day she used a different combination, the children then made different combinations, but did not use a systematic method to find out the exact number. The idea of combining just one T-shirt with each pair of shorts to find out the number of outfits that could be made with that T-shirt did not seem to occur to the deaf children as often as it occurred to the hearing children. A second type of error, often observed with hearing children too, was to add the number of T-shirts and shorts.

It is difficult to interpret the results observed with deaf children. The gap between the percentage of correct solutions to isomorphism-of-measures and product-of-measures problems is the same for hearing and deaf children, but the deaf children were considerably behind the hearing children in isomorphism-of-measures problems. We hypothesized that this could be due to their counting skills being less developed than that of the hearing children – rather than their logical understanding of correspondences – because their understanding was at ceiling in the non-computational, relational problems. If the same were true of product-of-measures problems – that is, if the deaf children understood the logic as well as the hearing children – there should be no reason for a further delay in producing correct responses to product-of-measures problems, because the numbers in the two types of problems were in the same counting range. However, it was quite clearly difficult to explain the problem to the deaf children. It is quite possible that a well-designed intervention using visual displays for the instruction would produce significant improvements in the deaf children's performance. In the last section of this chapter we describe the method that was used in our intervention programme for deaf children to support their analysis of product-of-measures problems.

We will now consider the representation of multiplicative reasoning problems.

Representing multiplicative reasoning problems

Concerning the studies of how signs used to represent the problem information affect children's solution to additive reasoning problems, our review showed that children perform differently when given analogue or symbolic representations to work out the solution. Unfortunately, there is a paucity of studies on how different ways of representing the information in multiplicative reasoning problems affect children's level of success in problem-solving. It has been established both with hearing (Correa, 1994) and with deaf children (Nunes and Moreno, 1997) that children are more successful when they have analogue representations than when they do not, but further studies are clearly needed.

Gravemeijer (1997) argues that the type of analogue representation used during problem-solving also matters. He proposed that using blocks to solve division problems may not be very helpful, because the blocks represent different objects at different moments during the solution process.

Imagine, for example, how blocks would be used to represent the solution to this problem: 'The teacher has 29 CDs. She is arranging them in boxes that hold 6 CDs each, in order to sell them at the school fair. How many boxes can she fill?' A child could take 29 blocks to represent the CDs. The child would then form groups of 6 blocks. Each group of 6 blocks represents a box. So the *blocks* start out representing CDs but a *group of blocks* represents a box. There are 5 blocks left, which continue to represent CDs; they do not represent a box because they would not fill a box.

In contrast, a similar problem would be interpreted differently: 'The teacher has 29 CDs. She is arranging them in boxes that hold 6 CDs each, in order to put them away. How many boxes does she need?' In this case, the 5 blocks left would represent one more box, because the teacher would still need the box to hold the 5 CDs.

Gravemeijer suggested that – because of this shift in the meaning of the blocks during problem-solving – children benefit from the use of representations that are more figurative, at least in the initial stages of instruction. Our investigation of problem-solving with deaf children confirms his hypothesis. We (Nunes and Moreno, 1998a) found that deaf children were more successful using analogue representations of a figurative type – for example, cut-out drawings of objects – than using blocks or Unifix cubes.

The coordination of analogue and symbolic representations, using numbers, has not been investigated systematically in the context of multiplicative reasoning. Our intervention programme for additive reasoning involved providing children with a number line in order to help them make a connection between analogue and symbolic representations. However, a number line may not be appropriate to represent multiplicative reasoning problems, because the logic of multiplicative reasoning is the relation between variables, which is not represented easily with one number line. An appropriate representation should provide the children with ways of thinking about the relation between the variables in the problems.

Gravemeijer (1994, 1997) has shown that children spontaneously create *tables* in order to represent both variables in a problem. He gave children division problems with larger numbers to see how they would represent the information symbolically. One of the problems was: 'A ship was stranded on an island. The captain established that there were 4000 biscuits left in the storeroom. The crew consisted of 64 people. If each ate 3 biscuits a day, how many days would the supply last?' He observed that the children tended to make tables using numbers, where the number of biscuits that would be eaten over a certain period (1 day, 10 days) would be written next to the number of days. This allowed them to keep track of the values that were connected across the variables. Gravemeijer concluded that tables are useful symbolic representations of the children's own reasoning. He thus suggested that this might be taken into account in the design of instruction on multiplicative reasoning problems.

Other researchers (Schwartz, 1988) have suggested that graphs are also important sources of support and can help children make a connection between different aspects of multiplicative reasoning problems. However, research on this use of graphs is still missing.

In spite of the scarcity of research on how different ways of representing the problem affect solution, two lessons can be learned from the available studies. The first one is that not all analogue representations work as well when hearing or deaf children solve problems that involve multiplicative reasoning. Analogue representations that are figurative – cut-out drawings, diagrams – seem to work better than less figurative ones, like blocks. Second, because the logic of multiplicative reasoning is based on relations between variables, it is likely that the use of symbolic representations that make the relations between variables clear – such as tables – are more useful to children than a single number line when they try to represent their own reasoning. It is hypothesized that graphs may be used to extend the children's reasoning, but research on this is, to our knowledge, still missing. It seems worthwhile investigating the use of graphs with deaf children because of the visual nature of this type of representation.

An intervention programme for deaf children

When designing the intervention for multiplicative reasoning problems, we relied on the same general principles described previously in connection with the additive reasoning intervention. We wanted to give the deaf pupils opportunities to think about the logic of multiplicative problems, which, as seen earlier on, is learned by hearing pupils informally outside school but less well learned by deaf pupils. We also wanted to promote deaf pupils' access to information through visual representations, and help them make connections between analogue and symbolic representations. Thus presentation of problem information was at first through drawings, which the pupils could use during their problem-solving, but these were progressively coordinated with and later replaced by tables and graphs. As indicated earlier on, in Chapter 3, we did not carry out a separate analysis of the effects of the programme on each type of mathematical problem. The evaluation of the effectiveness of the programme will be discussed in Chapter 6, where effects on a standardized mathematics assessment are considered.

The programme was implemented by the same six teachers of the deaf and with the same 23 children, during the time scheduled for the teaching of mathematics, as a continuation of the activities described in previous chapters.

The first problems (Figures 5.2 to 5.4) stimulated the use of correspondences as the path to solution, by asking the children to draw elements to complete a picture and then give a numerical answer. Similar problems followed, with different numbers, which also introduced symbolic representations and made initial connections to tables.

Similarly, division problems were presented to encourage the children to use their sharing reasoning and show how it worked through visual representation and using figurative representations (Figures 5.5 and 5.7). Some of the problems (e.g. Figure 5.6) aim to lead the children to make connections across different aspects of the situation. For example, by asking how many bags can be filled with sweets and how many children would receive sweets if one bag were given to each child, the connection

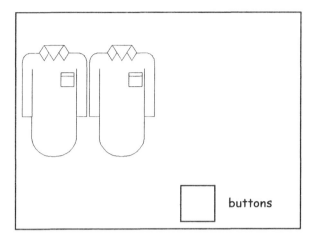

These shirts need 5 buttons each. Draw the buttons on each shirt.

How many buttons did you use for 2 shirts? Write your answer in the box.

Figure 5.2 A problem used to encourage the children to use correspondences as a problem-solving procedure.

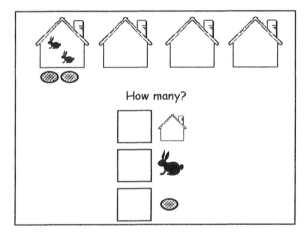

In each house in this street live 2 rabbits. Each rabbit eats one pellet of food a day.

Write in the boxes: How many houses are in this street?

How many rabbits live in this street?

How many pellets of food are eaten by all the rabbits altogether?

Figure 5.3 Making a connection between correspondences and symbols.

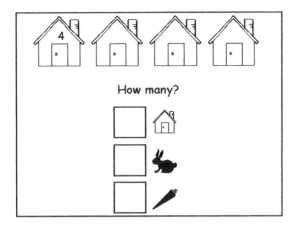

In each house in this street live 4 rabbits. They eat 2 carrots each per day. How many houses are in the street? How many rabbits live in this street? How many carrots do they eat altogether each day?

Figure 5.4 Making a connection between symbols and tables, with reduced support to the problem-solving process.

There are 4 children.
Share the 24 sweets fairly. Show the sweets each one gets.

How many sweets per child? Write your answer in the box.

Figure 5.5 A sharing problem to introduce the use of diagrams.

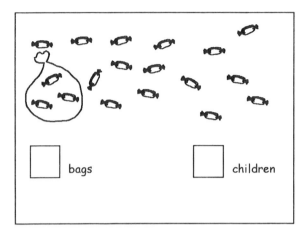

There are 18 sweets. Three sweets fit in a bag.

Can you put all the sweets in bags?

How many bags do you have? If you gave each bag to one child, how many children could get sweets? Write your answers in the boxes.

Figure 5.6 A sharing problem prompting the children to think about different connections between variables – between number of bags and number of sweets per child.

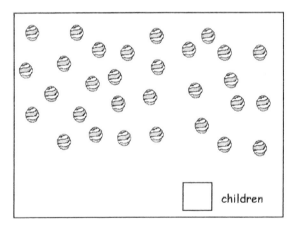

We are going to have a party. We have 30 marbles and we are going to give 5 to each child that comes.

How many children can come?

Write the number in the box.

Figure 5.7 A quotitive sharing problem the solution to which should be facilitated if it follows the problem in Figure 5.6.

between the bags and children is made. In the problem presented in Figure 5.7, the strategy of making lines around the quotas per child will be useful. If the children did not have this strategy before, by solving the problem in Figure 5.6 they might get this idea.

Inverse multiplicative situations, where one factor was missing, were also introduced initially through drawings, stimulating the use of visual representation of the problem solution (Figure 5.8) and later through tables.

It's the teacher's birthday and each child in his class gave him 2 flowers.

Now the teacher has 24 flowers.

How many children are there in the class?

Figure 5.8 An inverse multiplication problem where the ratio is known.

Tables were introduced more formally at a later point (Figures 5.9 to 5.13), allowing for the use of figurative representations alongside the tables at the start. The aim of provoking this connection between figurative and symbolic representations by means of tables was to facilitate the work with symbols. Initially the children were given the unit ratios (e.g. in Figure 5.9 they were given the ratio 1 child, 3 balloons). In problems presented later in the programme, they were asked to read non-unit ratios from tables and complete the tables. Less support is also offered in the drawings at later stages; thus more activity is required from the children. For example, in the problem presented in Figure 5.9 much structure is provided by the drawings: the unit ratio is given, the first part of the drawing is complete, and the children are drawn in correspondence with the numbers in the table. In contrast, in the problem presented in Figure 5.10, the information must be read from the table, the unit ratio is not given, and the vases are drawn randomly on the page, leaving the correspondence to the pupils' own resources. Later, tables and graphs were used simultaneously, with the aim of facilitating the mastery of this new form of symbolic representation.

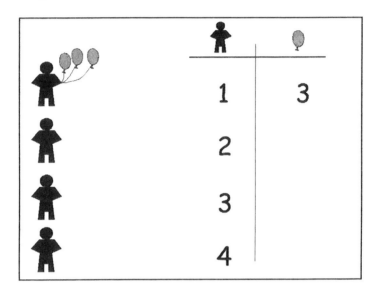

There are 4 children. Each child has 3 balloons.

Can you draw the rest of the balloons?

Can you finish the table?

Figure 5.9 Starting to work with tables.

Isomorphism-of-measures problems were made more complex by the introduction of multiple variables in the questions. For example, Figure 5.13 presents a problem where the children must keep in mind the connection between cartons of chocolate drink, number of cups that can be filled with each carton, and number of children that want a drink. These problems where multiple variables are introduced are more difficult than problems with one variable, but still easier than product-of-measures situations (Vergnaud, 1983).

Product-of-measures problems were introduced initially in a completely figurative way (Figure 5.14), by having the children concentrate on producing the combinations of forms and colours. The presentation

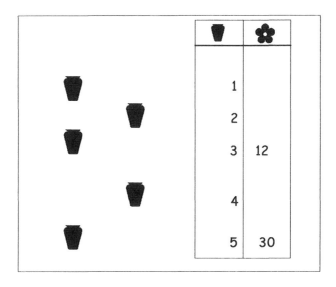

Can you fill in the rest of the table?

Figure 5.10 Introducing tables where the correspondence with the unit is not given.

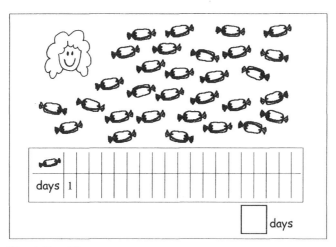

The girl has 30 sweets.

She wants to eat 2 a day.

How many days will it take her to eat all her sweets?

Fill in the table.

Figure 5.11 Strengthening the connection between analogue and symbolic representations using tables.

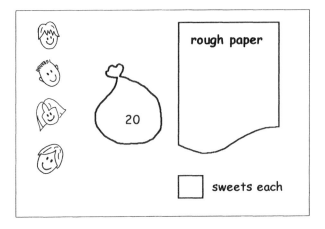

There are 4 children. The bag has 20 sweets.

If the sweets are shared fairly, how many sweets will each one get?

Write your answer in the box.

Figure 5.12 A sharing problem without the analogue representations.

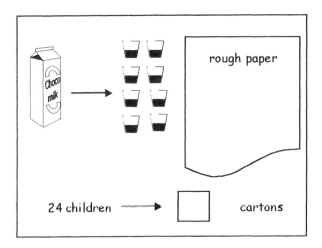

8 drinks can be poured from 1 carton.

24 children want a drink.

How many cartons do we need? Write your answer in the box.

Figure 5.13 A correspondence problem with three variables.

in a grid format facilitates solution and discussion if a child repeats a figure by using the same shape and the same colour. The grid support was reduced through a series of problems that became progressively less structured. At a later point the children were asked to invent their own problems.

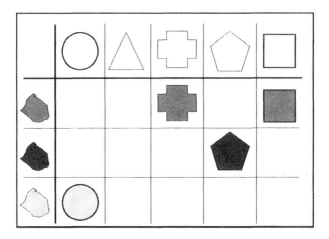

Complete the table, making different shapes with different colours.

Do not repeat figures that look exactly the same.

Figure 5.14 A matrix used towards product-of-measures problems.

Visual representation of multiplicative relations cannot adequately be done on a number line, which was the resource used for representing additive reasoning. Additive reasoning involves part–whole relations, and these can be represented on a single line. Because in multiplicative reasoning we deal with the relation between two variables, their relation can be represented numerically through tables (see Figures 5.9 to 5.11) or visually, using graphs. Figures 5.17 to 5.21 exemplify a sequence of tasks used in the representation of multiplicative relations by means of graphs. Figure 5.17 helps the children to start working with graphs by using analogue representations of the smiley faces that the children would receive for each page done correctly in their workbook. The children do not need to know anything about graphs to use this form of representation but are simply being prepared for the use of graphs. Figure 5.18 uses a more abstract representation of the numbers in the problem. However, this is still quite easy for the children because reading bar graphs is a small step from reading analogue representations: in a bar graph like the one used in Figure 5.18, each number on the vertical axis can clearly be connected

3 different shapes of hats for the clown.

3 different colours.

Complete the table combining the different shapes and colours.

How many different hats can you make? Write your answer in the box.

Figure 5.15 Starting to quantify product-of-measures problems.

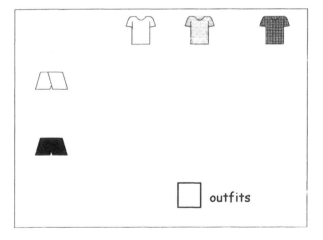

There are 3 T-shirts and 2 shorts.

How many different outfits can we make?

Write your answer in the box.

Figure 5.16 A product-of-measures problem with fewer cues.

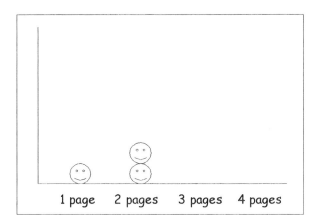

If you do one page of your book right, you get one smiley face. If you do 2 pages, you get 2 smiley faces. Complete the smiley faces for 3 pages and 4 pages.

Figure 5.17 Starting to draw graphs by using analogue representations.

to one balloon. Figure 5.19 introduces the demand of reading points. Note also that there is a further step in the work with this graph: each mark on the vertical axis represents two, rather than one, pence. Figures 5.20 and 5.21 were used to help the children make connections between the numerical and the visual representations of multiplicative relations. Figure 5.21 requires the children to read the information from a line, which is more demanding than reading points.

Further questions about linear representations were used to promote children's understanding of how this form of representation works. For example, one problem required them to draw two lines on the same graph, which represented the relation between number of pencils bought and their price in the different shops. The price of the pencils in one shop was higher than in the other. The children were asked to draw both lines and discuss why they were different. These analyses of line graphs in problems that the children can understand have the aims of supporting the children's reasoning about multiplicative situations and teaching them a variety of representations for multiplicative relations. It should be kept in mind that much information that we use in everyday life – from newspapers and magazines, for example – is presented by means of graphs. But we also see these analyses as a means to further development: we hypothesize that they prepare the children for learning about functions later on in school.

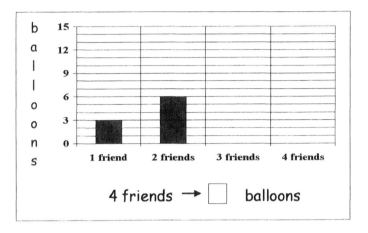

A girl is going to have a party. She is going to invite 4 friends. She is going
to give 3 balloons to each friend. Show on the graph how many balloons
for 3 and 4 friends. How many balloons does she have to buy for her 4
friends?

Figure 5.18 Coordinating graphs with information given in language.

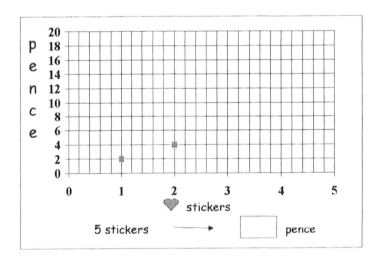

A girl bought 5 stickers. Find out on the graph how much she paid
for 1 and 2 stickers.

Mark the price for 3, 4 and 5 stickers on the graph. How much
money did she spend?

Figure 5.19 Getting information about multiplication problems from graphs.

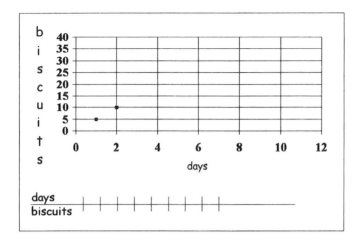

The teacher has a box with 40 biscuits. There are 5 children. Find out from the graph how many biscuits each child is getting per day.

In how many days will the biscuits finish? Show your answers on the table.

Figure 5.20 Coordinating graphs and tables.

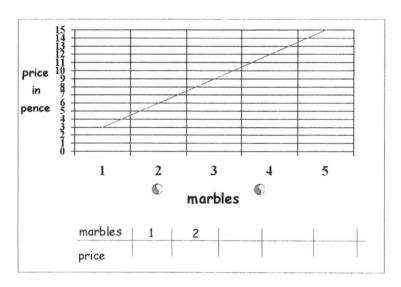

The graph shows the price of marbles in a shop. Fill in the table with the numbers of marbles and the prices.

Figure 5.21 Introducing the visual representation of line graphs in coordination with tables.

The complete series of multiplicative reasoning problems used in the programme contained 50 different items, which were varied in content, type of representation used for presentation of the information (analogue, table or graph), type of situation (isomorphism or product of measures), whether the problem was direct or inverse, and number of variables that the children were asked to consider.

Although the programme is not complete in the coverage of the issues that should be considered in multiplicative reasoning situations, it provided ample opportunity for the development of the core concepts and connections between different ways of representing information.

The assessment of the overall programme will be discussed in Chapter 6. However, it is worth mentioning that, similarly to what was observed with the materials on additive reasoning and number concepts in the Shop Task, both children and teachers enjoyed the work. Some teachers extended the work by creating large cut-out figures (with Velcro underneath), which the children used to demonstrate their solutions to the whole class. The problems offered the children many opportunities to have discussions about mathematical situations, which were most certainly useful in helping the children become more aware of the connections between variables. Some instances of excellent progress were observed in product of measures problems, with children showing a sudden understanding of the situation and offering to explain it to the other children.

To summarize, this chapter provided a brief description of the logic of multiplicative reasoning problems and an analysis of the children's actions that lead to the development of multiplicative reasoning. A simplified schema for classifying multiplicative situations was presented, which included two types of correspondence problems – *isomorphism of measures* and *product of measures*. The chapter also considered the different ways in which information can be presented when multiplicative reasoning problems are given to children. A sample of the problems used in our intervention programme was presented. These emphasized visual resources and representations that helped the children focus on the relation between variables, including analogue representations through drawings, and symbolic representations through tables and graphs.

CHAPTER 6

Teaching mathematics to deaf children: how the story began and the happy ending

In the last ten years I have been investigating how deaf children learn mathematics. I have often been asked: Why are you looking at deaf children's mathematics learning? Why not language? Why not literacy?

Implicit in these questions is the idea that it is reasonable to expect that deaf children have difficulty with language and literacy learning, but not with mathematics – and this is, relatively speaking, right. Powers et al. (1999) and Gregory (1998) have argued that, although there is a delay in the development of deaf children's mathematical competence, this is much less severe than their delay in literacy development. Powers et al. (1999) point out that teachers express much less concern with deaf children's mathematics learning than with their literacy learning. However, the review of quantitative studies presented in Chapter 1 showed that there are good reasons for being concerned with deaf children's mathematics achievement. In general, they perform less well than hearing children, and would be at a great disadvantage when competing for places in university courses and for jobs where mathematical knowledge is important.

Perhaps implicit in these questions is also the view that deaf children's difficulties in mathematics would be entirely solved if they could read the questions on exam papers and understand them. There is, as we have seen, a correlation between deaf children's reading ability and their success in problem-solving (Serrano Pau, 1995) – but, as discussed in Chapter 3, there is a lot more to consider in the teaching of mathematics to deaf children than whether they understand the language used in problem-solving.

My interest in deaf children's mathematics learning was provoked by observing some 8-year-old deaf children during a mathematics lesson. The children were being taught addition and subtraction number facts. The teacher put up a question on the board (for example, $8 + 3$ or $9 - 4$) and asked the children to read the question and provide the answer. If they provided the correct answer to the question, the teacher praised them enthusiastically and they enjoyed their success as if they had just won a point in a game. The rhythm of the lesson was quite slow because the children put up their hands to read the question and then put up their hands to provide the answer. I could picture myself as an 8-year-old in a mathematics lesson of this type, quickly working away at the solution on my fingers instead of trying to be called upon to read the question. Any child who did this would be able to score many points. But I did not see any children working out the solutions on their fingers in the class I was observing. They seemed to treat the whole thing almost like a guessing game.

I was puzzled. Why didn't the children try to work out the solution on their fingers? I had seen them counting earlier on during the same lesson, when they had been doing an assignment about even and odd numbers, so I knew that they could count and could have used counting to find out the answer. I am afraid that, to this day, I do not know why the children did not count. But they aroused my curiosity in such a way that I wanted to know more about deaf children's mathematics learning. Their difficulty in the task I was observing could not be explained by a failure to understand *language* – they were actually saying the questions themselves: 'eight add three', 'nine take away four'. So why didn't they try to figure out the answer?

My fascination with children's mathematical development up till then had been confined to hearing children's development. But then I wanted to know something about deaf children. I believed that the children I was watching were intelligent and I thought that they could be stimulated to learn more mathematics.

A search through the literature immediately showed that deaf youngsters were leaving school with less mathematical knowledge than they should. It also revealed many interesting threads that could be followed in pursuing reasons why deaf children might lag behind hearing children in mathematics. I will analyse these briefly in the first part of this chapter. The results of this analysis and our own investigations, described in the previous chapters, led me to hypothesize that it was possible to create an effective programme for promoting deaf children's mathematical development. This is the programme that was described throughout Chapters 2 to 5. The second part of this chapter describes the assessment of the programme.

Factors related to deaf children's mathematical competence

In Chapter 1 the possibility that there is a direct connection between hearing loss and difficulty in learning mathematics was discussed. The evidence from studies that searched for support for this direct connection is mostly negative. The studies (Wood, Wood, Griffiths and Howarth, 1986) showed that the correlation between the level of hearing loss and mathematical achievement is negligible. They could not account for deaf children's difficulties in mathematics. They also showed that an important number of severely and profoundly deaf pupils – about 15% – perform at average or above-average levels for their age in mathematics, a result that is inconsistent with the idea of a direct connection between deafness and difficulties in learning mathematics.

This negative evidence led us to hypothesize that deafness is a *risk factor* for difficulties in learning mathematics rather than a cause. If deafness were a cause of difficulty in learning mathematics, there would be no way round it. A risk factor means that there may be differences between hearing and deaf children's experiences and information processing preferences that make deaf children vulnerable to difficulty in learning mathematics (for a discussion of the difference between causes and risk factors, see Nunes and Moreno, 1998a). If these risk factors are dealt with, deaf children should be able to show considerable improvement in their mathematics learning. What could these risk factors be?

The preceding chapters in this book should place us in a better position to consider different hypotheses proposed in the literature. The insights gained from these chapters, and reviews of the literature not considered so far, will be used to analyse different hypotheses that have been raised about what factors place deaf children at risk for difficulties in mathematics learning. Chapters 2 to 5 considered mostly factors that related to the deaf children themselves, but some hypotheses in the literature relate to factors that are extrinsic to the children. It is thus important to search for an overview of the different hypotheses raised, and the evidence to support them, as we approach the end of this book. These hypotheses are considered briefly in the section that follows.

School placement of deaf pupils

One hypothesis – examined by Wood, Wood, Kingsmill, French and Howarth (1984) – was that the risk factors may not be inherent to the children but may result from the teaching that they are offered. Deaf children may be offered mathematics teaching that is different from the mathematics teaching offered to hearing children – and could therefore be learning less as a consequence of less successful teaching. This teaching could be less successful for many reasons; for example, the deaf children in special schools might be offered much more speech and language therapy than those in mainstream schools, and thus have less time for mathematics learning. Wood and his colleagues examined this hypothesis by comparing the progress made in mathematics by deaf pupils who attended special schools for the deaf and deaf pupils who attended mainstream schools. Although they found a significant effect of placement on the pupils' mathematics attainment, the difference between the two groups was not large enough to explain the difference between deaf and hearing pupils.

After reviewing the literature on this issue, Gregory (1998) concluded that educational placement cannot explain the difference between deaf and hearing pupils' attainment in mathematics.

Kluwin and Moores (1989) also considered the possibility that teaching might be a significant factor affecting deaf pupils' mathematics difficulties. They investigated the mathematics attainment of 215 deaf students in mainstream or special classes. They found that the pupils' background and the quality of teaching were significant factors affecting the deaf pupils' mathematics achievement, irrespective of placement. Placement by itself did not have an effect on achievement.

Taken together, these results suggest that the quality of teaching has an effect on deaf pupils' learning but that quality of teaching is not the same as placement in special or mainstream schools. They show that the difference between deaf and hearing pupils is not explained by a hypothetical difference in quality of mathematics teaching between mainstream and special schools.

The language of mathematics

Gregory (1998) suggested that if deaf pupils lack the language necessary to understand and solve mathematical questions, they will find it difficult to make progress in mathematics learning. She identified two ways in which lack of mathematical language could account for deaf pupils' difficulties. The first is that there is a specific vocabulary for mathematics – for example, hypotenuse, denominator, isosceles – and this vocabulary has to be learned. Although this is certainly a reason for difficulties with mathematics, hearing children also have to learn this specific vocabulary, so it is unlikely that the existence of a technical mathematical vocabulary could explain the differences in attainment between deaf and hearing pupils, particularly in primary school, when the specialized vocabulary is not yet used. The second reason is that some words, such as *difference*, *divide* and *similar*, have a more exact meaning when used in a mathematics lesson than in general conversation. Again, this is true, but it cannot explain the discrepancy in performance between hearing and deaf pupils, because both groups have to learn these specialized meanings in school.

Gregory's discussion does identify a specific difficulty that might be faced by deaf children who rely on BSL: there is no standardized mathematical vocabulary in BSL and the children might encounter different signs for the same mathematical ideas if they change schools. This is not a trivial issue, but it cannot account for the difference between deaf pupils who are educated orally and their hearing counterparts.

Thus it is certainly true that mathematics has a specialized language and that this may cause difficulties for pupils, but it is unlikely that the existence of a mathematical technical vocabulary explains the difference in achievement between deaf and hearing pupils.

The two hypotheses discussed so far do not seem to relate directly to deafness. Quality of teaching is important whether the pupils are hearing or deaf; it would only be a significant factor in producing differences between deaf and hearing children if it were shown that the quality of teaching offered to hearing children is largely better than that offered to deaf pupils, but this does not seem to be the case. Similarly, there is no reason for the specificity of mathematical language to be more of a problem for deaf than for hearing pupils, unless the teaching of mathematical vocabulary to deaf pupils is worse than that offered to hearing pupils.

Two other hypotheses are examined below, which are directly related to the psychology of deafness. These hypotheses suggest that different types of teaching may be necessary for deaf and hearing pupils, when the pupils' characteristics are considered.

Short-term memory restrictions

Research comparing deaf and hearing adults as well as children (Epstein, Hillegeist and Grafman, 1990; Marschark, 1993; Moreno, 1994) has shown that deaf people seem to be able to hold relatively less in their short-term memory than hearing people, particularly when the stimuli are presented in oral or sequential manner. It was argued in Chapter 3 that this is a plausible explanation for deaf children's difficulties with arithmetic story problems. So the design of instruction that aims at promoting their mathematical reasoning should avoid presenting information in ways that place the children at a disadvantage. This is what we tried to do when designing our intervention programme.

However, there is no evidence that shows that deaf children's weaker mathematical performance in a range of tasks is related to their short-term memory restrictions. To our knowledge, Moreno's (1994) study is the only one to provide direct evidence on this question – and her results do not support the hypothesis that deaf children's mathematics difficulties in a general assessment can be explained by their short-term memory restrictions. Moreno compared the performance of hearing and deaf children in a memory task, where the children were shown digits on a computer screen and later were asked to indicate whether a particular digit, presented by itself on the screen, had been part of the series of numbers that they had just seen. Different numbers of digits were presented, varying between 1 and 10. The children's scores were the number of digits in the longest series that they could recall accurately. The hearing children performed significantly better than the deaf children on this task. However, the deaf children's performance on this short-term memory task was not related to their performance on a standardized mathematics assessment, after controlling for age and non-verbal IQ. Moreno's findings confirm the poorer results displayed by deaf children on such tasks, but suggest that short-term memory restrictions cannot account for the difference between deaf and hearing children when a range of mathematical tasks is considered. As argued earlier on, in Chapter 2, mathematical tasks can and should be presented visually and spatially to the deaf in order to get round the possible disadvantage that would result from oral and sequential presentations. If this is done, short-term memory restrictions should not affect the deaf children's learning negatively. This could be the reason why short-term memory performance does not predict deaf children's mathematics achievement on a standardized test, after the required controls have been considered.

Lack of informal experiences

It has often been argued that deaf children might miss out on different things that happen around them, which would be picked up by hearing children as part of their incidental learning. Gregory (1998) suggested that they miss out on mathematical conversations. 'Hearing children hear mathematical talk almost from birth, "wait a minute", "that's too small for you now", "it's miles away". Most hearing children are also involved in mathematical talk themselves from early on, of which counting is a prime example' (Gregory, 1998: 123). Gregory suggested that deaf children may not have a similar exposure to mathematical conversation and that this might explain why they show a delay in learning the counting string. As analysed in Chapter 2, deaf children are as able in using counting as hearing children, when they are compared with hearing children who have a similar knowledge of the counting string, but they do show a delay in learning the counting string. So this suggests that lack of informal mathematical experiences might be a risk factor in the development of deaf children's mathematical competence.

The possibility that deaf children have less experience with some situations that provide a significant context for informal mathematics learning was considered in Chapters 3 to 5 in this book, where the use of different schemes of action to solve problems was investigated. The results suggest that there is a gap between hearing and deaf children's use of actions to solve problems and that this gap is often more severe when the actions have to be coordinated with counting. Such results are in agreement with the hypothesis of lack of experience, because in some situations many children show an understanding of the logic of the problem but cannot use this logic successfully to provide a numerical answer.

The hypothesis of lack of experience has been considered for at least half a century in the literature (e.g. Furth, 1966) and there is agreement that it is a plausible hypothesis. Furth and other researchers subsequently (e.g. Rapin, 1986; see Marshark, 1993, for a review) found a delay among deaf children in the development of some aspects of logical reasoning in children. For example, deaf children were found to show a delay on conservation tasks, where it is widely recognized that experience is an important developmental factor (e.g. Price-Williams et al., 1969). Thus lack of experience may have a wide-ranging effect on deaf children's logical and mathematical development.

Fortunately, lack of experience is exactly the type of risk factor that can be tackled in intervention programmes, particularly if there is sufficient research to identify which experiences are critical. This hypothesis was carefully considered in the design of the programme we implemented in the classrooms with the teachers. We tried to identify significant experiences for the development of specific mathematical concepts and ensure that these were included in the programme. So by choosing experiences that we knew from past research to be important for the development of mathematical reasoning, and by presenting the questions visually, we provided to the deaf children experiences that they could be lacking under conditions that facilitated their learning.

This brief review of the factors that have been considered as possible explanations for deaf children's mathematical difficulties can be interpreted as producing very encouraging results. They suggested the path to the design of a programme that could work. The programme should present information in a visual–spatial way and offer the children systematic exposure to experiences that they might lack and which are important for mathematics learning. We designed our programme, described in Chapters 2 to 5, with these principles in mind. The question is: Did it work?

The assessment of our intervention programme on deaf children's mathematics achievement

Intervention studies are a way to test hypotheses about causes in psychology. When correlational studies indicate that there might be a causal relation between two factors – for example, lack of specific experiences and success in learning mathematics – intervention studies can be used to test the hypothesis further (for a discussion of the importance of combining correlational and intervention studies, see Bradley and Bryant, 1983).

Intervention studies are also quite difficult to design in practice. The ideal situation – where a group of children is randomly assigned to the intervention group and a comparable group is assigned to the control group – is not easily implemented in schools, particularly when a special group of children, such as deaf children, is going to participate in the intervention. Teachers of the deaf in England are extremely motivated and dedicated. They are often eager to cooperate with research, and will work well beyond the confines of their time contracts, with the children's progress in mind. They would be much less eager if they were told that their children would not receive the benefits of an intervention that might promote their mathematics learning. Yet, without the research, it would be impossible to know whether the programme does in fact benefit the children's learning.

With the involvement of the teachers concerned, we (for a brief report, see Nunes and Moreno, 2002) decided to use a design to test the effectiveness of our intervention that did not involve the random assignment of the deaf children to a control or to an intervention group. We knew that it was necessary to have considerable amounts of information about what would be appropriate for deaf children before designing the information. So we first collected initial data on deaf children's performance on a standardized mathematics assessment in the schools where our project would be implemented later. This initial study, carried out with 82 deaf children, provided the information analysed in the preceding chapters about how the children solved problems, and their strengths and difficulties. So it helped us define more clearly the goals for our intervention programme. It also provided a baseline for the assessment of the effectiveness of the programme – we had collected data on a cohort that did not receive any intervention. The intervention programme was implemented with deaf children in the same schools and year groups one year later. Thus the mathematics achievement of the intervention group could be compared with the baseline data, which contained the scores of deaf children of the same age and attending the same schools in the previous year.

Method

The *participants* in this study comprise two groups: baseline pupils and project pupils. The *baseline pupils* were 68 children (from the 82 tested in the previous year) who were in the same year groups (3–6) as the pupils who received the intervention. The pupils in the intervention group, who will be referred to as *project pupils*, were 23 children in six different classes whose teachers agreed to implement the programme and participated in the meetings with the researchers during the period of the project.[1]

---

[1] One of the teachers went on maternity leave during the project. The project research assistant replaced her during this period, implementing the programme one hour per week during the period scheduled for mathematics lessons.

A *standardized mathematics assessment* was used to obtain the data on the children's mathematics performance. We thought that it was important to use a standardized assessment for two reasons. First, we did not want to run the risk of biasing the assessment to include materials that were part of the intervention but which would not be part of the children's mathematics curriculum. Second, standardized assessments allow for comparisons between different tests, which are used at different age levels. Children who are 8 years of age are given a test that is different in content from the test given to children who are 11. This is necessary because – as the children learn more mathematics – different questions become appropriate for assessing their competence. A standardized test contains information that allows the researcher to evaluate children of different ages according to the same scale, which is derived from the children's observed scores. We chose for our study the NFER-Nelson 7–1 Test Series, which was adequate for the age range of the pupils in the study. This series has different assessments for the different age levels, and allows for the conversion into a single scale of all the scores obtained by the children using different age-appropriate assessments. The test also has standardized scores, which take the children's age into account. This is important because the children who take the test designed for a particular age group – for example, the Mathematics 10 Test – vary to some extent in age. Suppose a child who is, for example, 9 years 8 months has the same score on the Mathematics 10 Test as another one, who is 10 years 6 months. Their scores – usually referred to as *raw* or *observed* scores – do not mean the same thing: the younger child's score might be slightly ahead of his or her age whereas the older child's score might be slightly behind his or her age. Standardized scores take these age differences into account and are obtained from a conversion table designed by the test's authors.

The *testing occasions* for the project and the baseline pupils were different. The *baseline pupils* were tested once, the year before the intervention was implemented in the classrooms. The *project pupils* were tested twice, once before the intervention – the pre-test – and a second time after the intervention – the post-test.

The *procedure* for using the tests is to administer them as a classroom testing. However, because the children were deaf, it was decided to use individual administration. So the children were seen individually by a trained researcher using the same language used by the schools with the children – English, BSL or SSE.

The number of pupils in each group according to the age-appropriate test taken is presented in Table 6.1. The numbers for the project group refer to post-test data. Note that the test used at pre-test will differ from the one used at post-test when the children had a birthday between the pre- and post-test. However, because the NFER provides scaled scores that are comparable across ages, the use of scale scores solves the problem of comparing pre- and post-test data when the children took a different test across occasions.

Table 6.1 Number of pupils in the project and baseline groups by age-appropriate test taken

| | Age-appropriate test taken | | | | |
	7 years	8 years	9 years	10 years	11 years
Project pupils	3	8	3	7	2
Baseline pupils	22	19	19	8	0

Brief description of the intervention

The intervention programme was administered by the teachers at their own pace, making use of time normally scheduled for mathematics lessons over two terms. During this period, the teachers participated in a series of meetings where the activities designed by the researchers were discussed with the teachers and modified, when necessary, in line with their suggestions. Once these modifications were agreed, all the teachers and children received the same materials.

The revised programme was organized in the booklets, which were used in the implementation of the programme in the classroom. The children's booklets contained pictures but no written instructions; these were included here in order to make it easier to present the problems to our readers. In the classrooms, the teachers conveyed the instructions to the pupils in the language normally used by them. We did not include written instructions because we wanted to avoid discouraging the children who could find reading instructions in itself a difficult task. The pupils were encouraged to use the booklets to work out their solutions by means of drawings and to use these in order to show the teacher and other pupils how they had found the answer. The examples presented in Chapters 2 to 5 were taken from these booklets. However, they do not compose the whole programme.

The teachers received a teacher book that contained the same pictures presented in the pupils' booklets, along with instructions explaining the question. The teachers were asked to give the instructions to their pupils in the pupils' language of instruction and to adapt the instructions to the pupils' linguistic knowledge. They were encouraged to introduce new items with practical materials if they felt this was needed in order to ensure that the situations were understood by the children.

All teachers were asked to attempt all the items with the pupils, even if they expected some of the concepts to be either too easy or too difficult for their pupils. They were also encouraged to use discussions amongst the pupils as the items were solved. They provided their own explanations to the pupils. The programme booklets worked as a starting point for them to work on everyday mathematical concepts and to promote the use of a variety of representations – analogue and symbolic. The booklets presented the information in visual–spatial form by using drawings, diagrams, number lines, tables and graphs, and presented story problems by having temporal sequences represented through pictures organized in spatial sequences, from left to right.

The programme was not envisaged as a replacement of the mathematics curriculum taught in the classroom. Its aim was to bring the deaf children's informal mathematical understanding to a level where it could offer a solid basis for learning the curriculum that they are taught in school. For this reason the programme was generally used once a week (sometimes twice), so that the teachers continued to implement the mathematics curriculum during the other lessons reserved for mathematics teaching.

Results

The *effect of the intervention* was assessed in two ways. The first analysis was a *comparison between the results obtained by the project pupils and those obtained by the baseline group*. For this comparison, we used the scale scores, which allow for comparisons across age levels.

We carried out two analyses, one comparing *the scores of the project pupils at pre-test with the scores of the baseline group* and the other comparing *the scores of the project pupils at post-test with the scores of the baseline group*. We had no reason to expect a significant difference between the project and the baseline pupils in the pre-test, because both groups of children had been drawn from the same schools. So our hypothesis is that the project and baseline pupils do not differ at pre-test. In contrast, if the intervention proved successful, the project pupils should perform significantly better than the baseline pupils in the post-test.

Table 6.2 shows the mean scale scores for the pupils in the baseline group and the project group at pre- and post-test.

Some aspects of these results merit comment. First, it is noted that the baseline pupils' scale scores improved with age (or year group) in school. This is an unexpected result because scores are adjusted precisely to allow for comparisons across age groups (just as children's IQ is not expected to increase with age, scale scores are not expected to increase with age).

Table 6.2 Mean scale scores in the NFER-Nelson for the baseline group and the project group in the pre- and post-tests by age-appropriate test taken

| | Age-appropriate test taken | | | |
	7 years	8 years	9 years	10 years
Baseline pupils	9.9	15.4	27.1	38.3
Project pupils at pre-test	11.4	17.0	27.0	33.0
Project pupils at post-test	22.3	29.3	32.8	43.5

The second aspect of the results to be noted is that there is very little difference between the project and baseline pupils when the project children's pre-test results are considered. This supports our hypothesis that the children in the baseline group did not differ from the project children before these received the intervention.

In contrast, at post-test the project pupils show consistently better results than the baseline group. This supports the hypothesis that the intervention helped them understand better the mathematical concepts that they were taught during the year. Figure 6.1 presents these results visually. It can be easily recognized that the baseline pupils do not differ from the project pupils at pre-test. However, at post-test the project pupils clearly perform better than the baseline pupils.

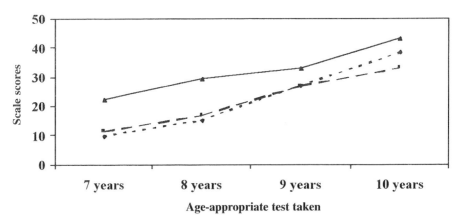

Key: - • - Baseline pupils — - Project pupils - pre-test —▲— Project pupils - post-test

Figure 6.1 Scale scores for each age group for the baseline pupils and the project pupils at pre- and post-test.

In order to test whether the differences observed were significant, we used a non-parametric statistic, the Mann–Whitney test, which is based on the ranks obtained by the pupils in each group. This was necessary because the scores were not distributed normally at each age level. In the pre-test, the mean rank for the baseline group was 44.8 and the mean rank for the project pupils was 47.6. This difference was not statistically significant ($p = 0.66$). In the post-test, the mean rank for the baseline group was 40.4 and the mean rank for the project pupils was 60.35. This difference, in contrast, was statistically significant ($p = 0.002$). So we can conclude that the project pupils did not differ from the baseline pupils at pre-test but outperformed the baseline pupils at post-test. This means that they improved significantly in their mathematics achievement during the time they were engaged in the programme.

There are no reasons to expect that these results could be explained by major policy changes taking place during the time when the project was carried out, because no changes occurred during this time. However, it must be stressed that the results are not due solely to the intervention, but to the combined effects of the instruction normally offered by the teachers plus those of the intervention. The programme did not replace the curriculum: our view is that it made the curriculum more accessible to the deaf pupils.

The effects that we documented cannot be explained in terms of the teaching time dedicated to mathematics that the children received, because the teachers did not increase the amount of time dedicated to teaching mathematics. The project materials were used during the time normally scheduled for mathematics lessons. No extra classroom helpers were made available during the project. Thus there is no reason to expect that the pupils would perform significantly better than the baseline group, other than their participation in the programme.

As in any other major intervention, where pupils participate in a large number of activities, it is not possible to say exactly what in the programme led to the significantly greater level of progress. The programme was designed with two of deaf children's needs in mind: the need for visual–spatial support in communication in the mathematics classroom, and the need for systematic teaching of concepts that hearing children might learn informally. The activities we designed were scrutinized by the participating teachers of the deaf, who made suggestions for the visual and linguistic presentation. The tasks were organized in groups that tackled the same concept from different perspectives and thus created for the children the opportunity of thinking about the same concept in different ways. The teachers encouraged the children to use drawings and diagrams to explain their answers, but the children did not have to invent these diagrams for themselves: the programme provided them with examples of drawings, diagrams, tables and graphs that could be used as tools for thinking and communicating about mathematics. The programme consisted exclusively of activities that involve reasoning: no time was dedicated to the teaching of algorithms. All of these aspects of the programme were new when traditional mathematics instruction at the time is considered.

Mathematics lessons, even for deaf pupils, seem to rely on language to a very large degree. Calculations are taught through the recall of verbally represented number bonds and rules for how to proceed. When there are misunderstandings in the teacher's explanations, there are few resources to support a discussion of the *mathematical ideas*. Visual means of representing relations between variables, such as tables and graphs, are typically not introduced in the context of problem-solving, as was the case in this intervention. At this age level, the curriculum includes only bar graphs, and the pupils are asked to read frequencies, without a consideration of how graphs show relations between variables. It is likely that all these differences jointly contributed to the positive impact of the programme. It is not possible to tease out the effects of the various cognitive aspects that were stimulated by the programme. The question of specific effects – what changes lead to what improvements – should be addressed in future research, such a fine-grained analysis would have been outside the aims of this intervention. Our aims were to maximize the learning opportunities for the deaf pupils.

We believe that many things change in a classroom when a programme such as this is introduced. Teachers may be energized by the novelty of the programme and may be more enthusiastic. They may spend more time in lesson preparation, and reflect more on the children's answers and how to create a discussion of concepts in the classroom. The positive effects that the programme may have had on the teachers would add to the effects of the programme per se.

It is possible that the programme was seen also by the children as bringing novelty into the classroom. Solving problems by means of drawings was not only an appropriate means of problem presentation for deaf children but also a great novelty. They had new ways of showing how they found their answers and new opportunities for discussion. Our own observations and the teachers' reports indicate that the pupils enjoyed working with the booklets. In one class the pupils clapped and showed great enthusiasm when the teacher asked them to go to their cupboards and bring out the booklets. In one class the pupils did not want to interrupt their work at lunch time, because they were too engaged in a discussion about the solution of a problem – a very unusual event in the teacher's experience of this group of pupils. Thus it is likely that there were *motivational effects* operating beyond the cognitive aims of the project.

We believe that the positive effects of this intervention should be attributed both to cognitive and to motivational factors. The *cognitive effects* are likely to be based both on the specific design for teaching the core concepts included in the programme and on the use of visual and spatial means of representation, which is in harmony with deaf children's information processing strengths. The instruction programme was carefully designed to make use of children's mathematical intuitions and to help them coordinate their informal knowledge with conventional mathematical tools – such as number words, number lines, tables and graphs. Drawings and diagrams were used both for their value as analogue representations and for the visual nature of the displays. The pupils seem to have found drawings and diagrams useful as a means of representing their ideas and working towards solutions. Teachers reported that their pupils, after starting to work with the project booklets, had begun to use drawings and diagrams at other moments in the mathematics lessons. Thus the motivational and cognitive aspects together seem to have contributed to the success of the programme. And it must be added that the programme would not have been successful if teachers and children had not enjoyed it.

Conclusion

There are, undoubtedly, many unanswered questions about what makes mathematics learning difficult for deaf children and what could make the teaching of mathematics to deaf children a more enjoyable and successful experience. Throughout the chapters the need for further research was emphasized. There is a scarcity of research on deaf preschoolers, and on the possibility that appropriate intervention before school might allow deaf children to start school with good informal mathematical knowledge and be ready to learn as well as hearing children. Intervention studies are a necessary tool to test causal hypotheses but also a necessary tool for the development and assessment of new approaches to teaching.

In spite of the gaps in our knowledge, this story does have a happy ending. From the insights gained through the review of the literature, the different studies we carried out, and especially through the participation of teachers and children in this teaching programme, we know that success in mathematics can be obtained by many more deaf children than would be expected without our intervention. It is hoped that this book will make it possible for more teachers and children to benefit from the programme.

References

Alibali MW, DiRusso AA (1999) The function of gesture in learning to count: More than keeping track. Cognitive Development 14:37–56.

Austin GF (1975) Knowledge of selected concepts obtained by an adolescent deaf population. American Annals of the Deaf 120:360–70.

Barham JC, Bishop A (1991) Mathematics and the deaf child. In: Durkin K, Shire B (eds) Language in Mathematics Education: Research and Practice. Buckingham: Open University Press, pp 179–88.

Blank M, Bridger WH (1966) Conceptual cross-modal transfer in deaf and hearing children. Child Development 37:29–38.

Braden JP (1992) Intellectual assessment of deaf and hard of hearing people: A quantitative and qualitative research synthesis. School Psychology Review 21:82–94.

Braden JP (1994) Deafness, Deprivation and IQ. New York: Plenum Press.

Bradley L, Bryant PE (1983) Categorising sounds and learning to read – a causal connection. Nature 301:419–521.

Briars DJ, Siegler R (1984) A featural analysis of preschoolers' counting knowledge. Developmental Psychology 20:607–18.

Brink J van den (1987) Children as arithmetic book authors. For the Learning of Mathematics 7:44–8.

Brissiaud R (1992) A tool for number construction: Finger symbol sets. In: Bideau J, Melijac C, Fisher J-P (eds) Pathways to Number: Children Developing Numerical Abilities. Hillsdale, NJ: Erlbaum, pp 41–67.

Brown JS, VanLehn K (1982) Towards a generative theory of 'bugs'. In: Carpenter TP, Moser JM, Romberg TA (eds) Addition and Subtraction: A Cognitive Perspective. Hillsdale, NJ: Erlbaum, pp 117–35.

Brown M (1981) Number operations. In: Hart K (ed) Children's Understanding of Mathematics: 11–16. Windsor: NFER-Nelson, pp 23–47.

Bryant PE (1985) The distinction between knowing when to do a sum and knowing how to do it. Educational Psychology 5:207–15.

Butterworth B (1999) The Mathematical Brain. London: Macmillan.

Carpenter TP, Moser JM (1982) The development of addition and subtraction problem solving. In: Carpenter TP, Moser JM, Romberg TA (eds) Addition and Subtraction: A Cognitive Perspective. Hillsdale, NJ: Erlbaum, pp 10–24.

Conrad R (1979) The Deaf School Child: Language and Cognitive Function. London: Harper & Row.

Correa J (1994) Young children's understanding of the division concept. Department of Experimental Psychology, University of Oxford.

Correa J, Nunes T, Bryant P (1998) Young children's understanding of division: The relationship between division terms in a noncomputational task. Journal of Educational Psychology 90:321–9.

Davis GE, Hunting RP (1990) Spontaneous partitioning: Preschoolers and discrete items. Educational Studies in Mathematics 21:367–74.

Davis GE, Pepper KL (1992) Mathematical problem solving by pre-school children. Educational Studies in Mathematics 23:397–415.

Davis GE, Pitkethly A (1990) Cognitive aspects of sharing. Journal for Research in Mathematics Education 21:145–53.

Dehaene S (1997) The Number Sense. Oxford: Oxford University Press.

Emmorey K (1998) The impact of sign language use on visuospatial cognition. In: Marschark M, Clark MD (eds) Psychological Perspectives on Deafness, Vol 2. Mahwah, NJ: Erlbaum, pp 19–51.

Epstein KI, Hillegeist EG, Grafman J (1990) Number processing in deaf college students. American Annals of the Deaf 139:336–47.

Fischbein E, Deri M, Nello M, Marino M (1985) The role of implicit models in solving verbal problems in multiplication and division. Journal for Research in Mathematics Education 16:3–17.

Fridriksson T, Stewart D (1988) From the concrete to the abstract: Mathematics for deaf children. American Annals of the Deaf 133:51–5.

Frostad P (1996) Mathematical achievement of hearing impaired students in Norway. European Journal of Special Needs Education 11:67–81.

Frostad P, Ahlberg A (1999) Solving story-based arithmetic problems: Achievement of children with hearing impairment and their interpretation of meaning. Journal of Deaf Studies and Deaf Education 4:283–98.

Frydman O (1990) The Role of Correspondence in the Development of Number Based Strategies in Young Children. Unpublished Doctoral thesis, University of Oxford.

Frydman O, Bryant PE (1988) Sharing and the understanding of number equivalence by young children. Cognitive Development 3:323–39.

Fuentes M (1999) La comprensión de numerales en niños sordos (Deaf children's understanding of numerals). Unpublished Doctoral thesis, University of Barcelona, Barcelona.

Fuentes M, Tolchinsky L (1999) La influencia de la lengua en el aprendizaje de los numerales: El caso de los niños sordos profundos prelocutivos (Linguistic influences on the learning of numerals: The case of prelingually profoundly deaf children). Revista de Logopedia, Foniatría y Audiología XIX:19–32.

Fuentes M, Tolchinsky L (2004) The subsystem of numerals in Catalan Sign Language: Description and examples from a psycholinguistic study. Sign Language Studies (in press).

Furth HG (1966) Thinking Without Language. New York: Free Press.

Furth H (1971) Linguistic deficiency and thinking: Research with deaf subjects 1964–1969. Psychological Review 76:58–72.

Fuson KC (1988) Children's Counting and Concepts of Number. New York: Springer.

Gallistel CR, Gelman R (1992) Preverbal and verbal counting and computation. Cognition 44:43–74.

Gay J, Cole M (1967) The New Mathematics and an Old Culture. A Study of Learning among the Kpelle of Liberia. New York: Holt, Rhinehart & Winston.

Geary D (1994) Children's Mathematical Development: Research and Practical Applications. Washington, DC: American Psychological Association.

Gelman R, Gallistel CR (1978) The Child's Understanding of Number. Cambridge, MA: Harvard University Press.

Gelman R, Meck E (1983) Preschoolers' counting: Principles before skill. Cognition 13:343–59.

Gelman R, Meck E (1986) The notion of principle: The case of counting. In: Hiebert J (ed) Conceptual and Procedural Knowledge: The Case of Mathematics. Hillsdale, NJ: Erlbaum, pp 29–58.

Ginsburg H (1977) Children's Arithmetic: The Learning Process. New York: Van Nostrand Reinhold.

Ginsburg HP, Klein A, Starkey P (1998) The development of children's mathematical thinking: Connecting research with practice. In: Damon W, Siegel IE, Renninger AA (eds) Handbook of Child Psychology. Child Psychology in Practice, Vol 4. New York: John Wiley, pp 401–76.

Goldin-Meadow S (2003) The Resilience of Language: What Gesture Creation in Deaf Children Can Tell Us About How All Children Learn Language. New York: Psychology Press.

Gravemeijer KPE (1994) Developing Realist Mathematics Education. Utrecht: Utrecht University Press.

Gravemeijer K (1997) Mediating between concrete and abstract. In: Nunes T, Bryant P (eds) Learning and Teaching Mathematics. An International Perspective. Hove: Psychology Press, pp 315–46.

Gravemeijer K, Heuvel M van den, Streefland L (1990) Contexts, Free Productions, Tests and Geometry in Realistic Mathematics Education. State University of Utrecht, Utrecht.

Greer B (1992) Multiplication and division as models of situations. In: Grouws DA (ed) Handbook of Research on Mathematics Teaching and Learning. New York: Macmillan, pp 276–95.

Greer B (1994) Extending the meaning of multiplication and division. In: Harel G, Confrey J (eds) The Development of Multiplicative Reasoning in the Learning of Mathematics. Albany, NY: State University of New York Press, pp 61–88.

Grégoire J, Van Niewenhoven C (1995) Counting at nursery school and primary school: Toward an instrument for diagnostic assessment. European Journal of Psychology of Education 10:61–75.

Gregory S (1998) Mathematics and deaf children. In: Gregory S, Knight P, McCracken, Powers S, Watson L (eds) Issues in Deaf Education. London: David Fulton, pp 119–26.

Groen GJ, Parkman JM (1972) A chronometric analysis of simple addition. Psychological Review 79:329–43.

Groen G, Resnick L (1977) Can preschool children invent addition algorithms? Journal of Educational Psychology 69:645–52.

Harel G, Confrey J (1994) The Development of Multiplicative Reasoning in the Learning of Mathematics. Albany, NY: State University of New York Press.

Hart K (1981) Ratio and proportion. In: Hart K (ed) Children's Understanding of Mathematics: 11–16. London: John Murray, pp 88–101.

Hart K (1984) Ratio: children's strategies and errors. A report of the strategies and errors in secondary mathematics project. Windsor: NFER-Nelson.

Hermelin B, O'Connor N (1975) The Recall of Digits by Normal, Deaf and Autistic Children. British Journal of Psychology 66:203–9.

Hine WD (1970) The attainment of children with partial hearing. Journal of the British Association of Teachers of the Deaf 68:129–35.

Hitch GJ, Arnold P, Philips LJ (1983) Cognitive processes in deaf children's arithmetic. British Journal of Psychology 74:429–37.

Houde O (1997) Numerical development: from the infant to the child. Wynn's (1992) paradigm in 2- and 3-year olds. Cognitive Development 12:373–91.

Hoyles C, Noss R (1992) A pedagogy for mathematical microworlds. Educational Studies in Mathematics 23:31–57.

Hughes M (1986) Children and Number. Oxford: Blackwell Science.

Hyde M, Zevenbergen R, Power D (2003) Deaf and hard of hearing students' performance on arithmetic word problems. American Annals of the Deaf 148:56–64.

Inhelder B, Piaget J (1958) The Growth of Logical Thinking from Childhood to Adolescence. New York: Basic Books.

Kamii M (1980) Children's Graphic Representation of Numerical Concepts. A Developmental Study. Unpublished doctoral dissertation, Harvard University.

Kelly RR, Lang HG, Mousley K, Davis SM (2002) Deaf college students' comprehension of relational language in arithmetic compare problems. Journal of Deaf Studies and Deaf Education 8:120–32.

Kelly RR, Lang HG, Pagliaro CM (2003) Mathematics word problem solving for deaf students: A survey of practices in Grades 6–12. Journal of Deaf Studies and Deaf Education 8:104–19.

Kluwin TN, Moores DF (1989) Mathematics achievement of hearing impaired adolescents in different placements. Exceptional Children 55:327–35.

Kornilaki E (1994) The Understanding of the Numeration System Among Preschool Children. Unpublished MSc thesis, Department of Child Development and Primary Education, University of London.

Kornilaki E (1999) Young Children's Understanding of Multiplicative Concepts. A Psychological Approach. London: Institute of Education, University of London.

Leybaert J, Van Cutsem M-N (2002) Counting in sign language. Journal of Experimental Child Psychology 81:482–501.

Lillo-Martin D (1999) Modality effects and modularity in language acquisition: The acquisition of American Sign Language. In: Ritchie WC, Bhatia TK (eds) The Handbook of Child Language Acquisition. New York: Academic Press, pp 531–67.

Marschark M (1993) Psychological Development of Deaf Children. New York: Oxford University Press.

Marschark M, Mayer TS (1998) Mental representation and memory in deaf adults and children. In: Marschark M, Clark MD (eds) Psychological Perspectives on Deafness, Vol 2. Mahwah, NJ: Erlbaum, pp 53–77.

Miller KF, Stigler JW (1987) Counting in Chinese: Cultural variation in a basic skill. Cognitive Development 2:279–305.

Miura IT, Kim CC, Chang C-M, Okamoto Y (1988) Effects of language characteristics on children's cognitive representation of number: Cross-national comparisons. Child Development 59:1445–50.

Miura IT, Okamoto Y, Kim CC, Chang C-M, Steere M, Fayol M (1994) Comparisons of children's cognitive representation of number: China, France, Japan, Korea, Sweden and the United States. International Journal of Behavioural Development 17:401–11.

Moreno C (1994) The Implementation of a Realistic Mathematics Education Programme in a Special School for the Deaf. Unpublished Master's thesis, Institute of Education, University of London.

Moreno C (2000) Predictors of Mathematics Attainment in Hearing Impaired Children. Unpublished PhD thesis, Institute of Education, University of London.

Mulhern G, Budge A (1993) A chronometric study of mental addition in profoundly deaf children. Applied Cognitive Psychology 7:53–62.

National Council of Teachers of the Deaf Research Committee (1957) The teaching of arithmetic in schools for the deaf. The Teacher of the Deaf 151:165–72.

Nesher P (1988) Multiplicative school word problems: Theoretical approaches and empirical findings. In: Hiebert J, Behr M (eds) Number Concepts and Operations in the Middle Grades. Hillsdale, NJ: Erlbaum, pp 19–40.

Newport EL, Meier RP (1985) The acquisition of American Sign Language. In: Slobin DI (ed) The Cross-linguistic Study of Language Acquisition: Vol 1. The Data. Hillsdale, NJ: Erlbaum.

Noss R, Hoyles C (1996) Windows on Mathematical Meaning: Learning Cultures and Computers. Dordrecht: Kluwer.

Nunes T (1995) Number signing and arithmetic in deaf children. Report presented to the Nuffield Foundation (Grant number AT/259 [EDU]), London.

Nunes T (1997) Systems of signs and mathematical reasoning. In: Nunes T, Bryant P (eds) Learning and Teaching Mathematics. An International Perspective. Hove: Psychology Press, pp 29–44.

Nunes T, Bryant P (1991) Correspondência: Um esquema quantitativo básico. (One-to-one correspondence as a basic quantitative scheme). Psicologia: Teoria e Pesquisa 7:273–84.

Nunes T, Bryant P (1996) Children Doing Mathematics. Oxford: Blackwell.

Nunes T, Moreno C (1996) Solving word problems with different mediators: How do deaf children perform? Paper presented at the International Group for the Psychology of Mathematics Education. Valencia, Spain.

Nunes T, Moreno C (1997) Solving word problems with different ways of representing the task. Equals Mathematics and Special Educational Needs 2:15–17.

Nunes T, Moreno C (1998a) Is hearing impairment a cause of difficulties in learning mathematics? In: Donlan C (ed) The Development of Mathematical Skills. Hove: Psychology Press, pp 227–54.

Nunes T, Moreno C (1998b) The signed algorithm and its bugs. Educational Studies in Mathematics 35:85–92.

Nunes T, Moreno C (2002) An intervention program to promote deaf pupils' achievement in numeracy. Journal of Deaf Studies and Deaf Education 7:120–33.

Nunes T, Schliemann AD, Carraher DW (1993) Street Mathematics and School Mathematics. New York: Cambridge University Press.

Nunes Carraher T (1982) O desenvolvimento mental e o sistema numérico decimal. In: Carraher TN (ed) Aprender Pensando: Contribuições da Psicologia Cognitiva para a Educação. Editora Vozes, Petrópolis, Brazil, pp 51–68.

Nunes Carraher T (1985) The decimal system: Understanding and notation. In: Proceedings of the 9th International Conference for the Psychology of Mathematics Education, Vol 1. Utrecht: Research Group on Mathematics Education and Educational Computer Centre, State University of Utrecht, pp 288–303.

Nunes Carraher T, Schliemann AD (1983) Fracasso escolar: Uma questão social (School failure: A social problem). Cadernos de Pesquisa 45:3–19.

Nunes Carraher T, Schliemann AD (1990) Knowledge of the numeration system among preschoolers. In: Steffe LP, Wood T (eds) Transforming Children's Mathematics Education. Hillsdale, NJ: Erlbaum, pp 135–41.

O'Connor N, Hermelin B (1972) Seeing and hearing and space and time. Perception and Psychophysics 11:46–8.

Pascual-Leone J (1970) A mathematical model for the transition rule in Piaget's developmental stages. Acta Psychologica 32:301–45.

Perret J-F (1985) Comprendre l'écriture des nombers. Berne: Peter Lang.

Petitto L (2000) The acquisition of natural signed languages: Lessons in the nature of human language and its biological foundations. In: Chamberlain C, Morford JP, Mayberry R (eds) Language Acquisition by Eye. Mahwah, NJ: Erlbaum, pp 41–50.

Piaget J (1952) The Child's Conception of Number. London: Routledge & Kegan Paul.

Power RD, Dal Martelo MF (1990) The dictation of Italian numerals. Language and Cognitive Processes 5:237–54.

Powers S, Gregory S, Lynas W, McCracken W, Watson L, Boulton A, Harris D (1999) A Review of Good Practice in Deaf Education. London: Report to the Royal National Institute for Deaf People; The Universities of Birmingham and Manchester.

Price-Williams D, Gordon W, Ramirez M (1969) Skill and conversation: A study of pottery-making children. Developmental Psychology 1:769–79.

Rapin I (1986) Helping deaf children acquire language: Lessons from the past. International Journal of Paediatric Otorhinolaryngology 11:213–23.

Resnick LB (1982) Syntax and semantics in learning to subtract. In: Carpenter TP, Moser JM, Romberg TA (eds) Addition and Subtraction: A Cognitive Perspective. Hillsdale, NJ: Erlbaum, pp 136–55.

Riley M, Greeno JG, Heller JI (1983) Development of children's problem solving ability in arithmetic. In: Ginsburg H (ed) The Development of Mathematical Thinking. New York: Academic Press, pp 153–96.

Saxe GB, Guberman SR, Gearhart M (1987) Social processes in early number development. Monographs of the Society for Research in Child Development 52:(2, Serial No 216).

Schwartz J (1988) Intensive quantity and referent transforming arithmetic operations. In: Hiebert J, Behr M (eds) Number Concepts and Operations in the Middle Grades. Hillsdale, NJ: Erlbaum, pp 41–52.

Secada W (1984) Counting in sign: The Number String, Accuracy and Use. Unpublished PhD thesis, Northwestern University, Evanston, IL, USA.

Seron X, Fayol M (1994) Number transcoding in children: A functional analysis. British Journal of Developmental Psychology 12:281–300.

Serrano Pau C (1995) The deaf child and solving problems in arithmetic. The importance of comprehensive reading. American Annals of the Deaf 140:287–90.

Silva ZHM (1993) A compreensão o da escrita numérica pela criança. Paper presented at the ISSBD Conference, Recife, Brazil.

Sinclair H, Sinclair A (1986) Children's mastery of written numerals and the construction of basic number concepts. In: Hiebert J (ed) Conceptual and Procedural Knowledge: The Case of Mathematics. Hillsdale, NJ: Erlbaum, pp 59–74.

Steffe LP, Thompson PW, Richards J (1982) Children's counting in arithmetical problem solving. In: Carpenter TP, Moser JM, Romberg TA (eds) Addition and Subtraction: A Cognitive Perspective. Hillsdale, NJ: Erlbaum, pp 83–96.

Todman J, Seedhouse E (1994) Visual-action code processing by deaf and hearing children. Language and Cognitive Processes 4:129–41.

Traxler CB (2000) The Stanford Achievement Test, 9th Edition: National norming and performance standards for deaf and hard-of-hearing students. Journal of Deaf Studies and Deaf Education 5:337–48.

Vergnaud G (1982) A classification of cognitive tasks and operations of thought involved in addition and subtraction problems. In: Carpenter TP, Moser JM, Romberg TA (eds) Addition and Subtraction: A Cognitive Perspective. Hillsdale, NJ: Erlbaum, pp 60–7.

Vergnaud G (1983) Multiplicative structures. In: Lesh R, Landau M (eds) Acquisition of Mathematics Concepts and Processes. London: Academic Press, pp 128–75.

Vergnaud G (1988) Multiplicative structures. In: Hiebert J, Behr M (eds) Number Concepts and Operations in the Middle Grades. Reston, VA: National Council of Teachers of Mathematics, pp 141–61.

Vergnaud G (1997) The nature of mathematical concepts. In: Nunes T, Bryant P (eds) Learning and Teaching Mathematics. An International Perspective. Hove: Psychology Press, pp 1–28.

Vernon PE, Miller KM (1976) Graded Arithmetic-Mathematics Test. Sevenoaks (UK): Hodder & Stoughton.

Vershaffel L, De Corte E (1997) Word problems: A vehicle for promoting authentic mathematical understanding and problem solving in the primary school? In: Nunes T, Bryant P (eds) Learning and Teaching Mathematics. An International Perspective. Hove: Psychology Press, pp 69–97.

Wang Y-J (1995) A Study of Chinese Children's Counting and Their Understanding of the Numeration System. Institute of Education, University of London.

Wakeley A, Rivera S, Langer J (2000) Can young infants add and subtract? Child Development 71:1525–34.

Wechsler D (1974) Wechsler Intelligence Scale for Children – Revised. Windsor: National Foundation for Educational Research.

Wollman DC (1965) The attainments in English and arithmetic of secondary school pupils with impaired hearing. The Teacher of the Deaf 159:121–9.

Wood D, Wood H, Howarth P (1983) Mathematical abilities of deaf school leavers. British Journal of Developmental Psychology 1:67–73.

Wood D, Wood H, Griffiths A, Howarth I (1986) Teaching and Talking with Deaf Children. Chichester: John Wiley.

Wood HA, Wood DJ, Kingsmill MC, French JRW, Howarth P (1984) The mathematical achievement of deaf children from different educational environments. British Journal of Educational Psychology 54:254–64.

Wright R (1994) Commutativity in Word Problem Situations. Paper presented at the Developmental Section of the BPS, Portsmouth, UK.

Wynn K (1992) Addition and subtraction by human infants. Nature 358:749–50.

Young RM, O'Shea T (1981) Errors in children's subtraction. Cognitive Science 5:153–77.

Zarfaty Y, Nunes T, Bryant P (2004) The performance of young deaf children in spatial and temporal number tasks. Journal of Deaf Studies and Deaf Education 9: (in press).

Index

Page numbers in **bold** type refer to figures, those in *italics* to tables

addition
    commutativity of 38, 39, 46, 72
    direct 55–8, 59–60, 62, **69**, **70**
    inverse 56–8, 59–60, 62, 63, **72**
    problems in 51
    repeated, multiplication as 112–13
additive composition 85–6
    assessing understanding of 91–5
    deaf *v.* hearing children 91–2
    logic of 107–11
    promoting understanding of 95–7
    and reading and writing numbers 107
additive reasoning 50–84
    core of 51
age, arithmetic
    v. chronological 2–3
    deaf *v.* hearing children 3–4, 22–3
algorithms, *see* signed algorithm
American Sign Language 33
analogue representation in problem
    solving 90–1, 94, 97, **98–100**
    division 126
    hidden addend problems 94–5, **100**
    multiplication 133–4, **134–5**

Belgian French Sign Language 33
Box Task 52–3
British Sign Language (BSL) 30, 104
    counting in 30–2, 33
    no mathematical vocabulary in 152
bugs, *see* errors
bus story 64–7

Cartesian problems, *see* product of
    measures problems

cartoons 67–72
Catalan Sign Language (CSL) 103–4
change problems 52–72
    change decrease *56*
    change increase *56*
    deaf *v.* hearing children 58–9
    description 52
    numerical information representation
        60–4
    representing information in 60–72
    sequence of events representation
        64–72
    types of, requiring different thought
        operations 55–60
    see also change-unknown problems
Change Task **54**, 55
change-unknown problems 62–3, 63, 69,
    71, 74
coding, visual *v.* phonological 25
cognitive effects, of intervention pro-
    gramme 162–3
combine problems 72–7
commutativity
    of addition 38, 39, 46, 72
    of multiplication 116–17
compare problems 78–81
    representation through drawings
        79–81, **82**, **83**
competence, mathematical,
    see mathematical competence
concatenation 102, **103**
Concept of Units Task *88*
concepts, mathematical,
    see mathematical concepts
conventions, mathematical 18

173

correlational studies/analysis 8–11,
    107–8, 109–10
correspondence 135–7
    one-to-many 89, 90, 114
    one-to-one 35–6, 101, 113
    and ratio 115
    understanding of, and multiplicative
        reasoning 115
'count all' 39
counting
    in British Sign Language (BSL) 30–2,
        33
    checking others 17
    counting down 45
    creative 22, 36–40
    with different types of units 86–8
    errors in 29, 30
    finger-counting 40–2
    of objects 35–6
    phonological confusions 29, 30
    systems of 18, 28, 85
counting range, matching for 34
counting string 28–36, 48
    deaf v. hearing children 59–60
    flexibility of knowledge of 34–5
    irregularities in 28
    learning 33–4
    oral 29–30
counting systems 18, 28, 85

deaf children of deaf parents, sign
    language 7
deaf children of hearing parents
    concept of units 88
    language 7
deafness
    causes of, and mathematical
        achievement 8–9
    delay in diagnosis 7
    and intellectual development 9–10
    level of, and mathematics achievement
        8–9
direct (additive) problems 55–8, 62, 69,
    70
    v. inverse problems 56, 59–60
direct (multiplicative) problems 119,
    120
division 121–7, 135–9
    age at which taught 112

deaf v. hearing children 122
direct 121–3
fixed ratios 121, 126
inverse 121, 123–6
partitive 123, 124–6
quotitive 124–6, 138
relationship between variables 121,
    123
see also sharing

errors
    in arithmetic 44–6
    in counting 29, 30
    failure to carry 44, 45, 46
    lexical 105, 106
    phonological confusions 29, 30
    in signed algorithm 45–6
    skipping five 45–6
    syntactic 105, 106
    taking smaller from bigger 44, 45
    in visually similar letters 25
experience, mathematical
    lack of 19–20, 154–5
    see also mathematical knowledge,
        informal

finger-counting 40–2
fixed ratios
    in division 121, 126
    in multiplication 114, 119
    see also ratio

graphs 134, 135, 143–7

hidden addend problems 75
    analogue representations 94–5, 100

information
    numerical, representation of 60–4
    representation of 18–19
information processing 58–9, 60
intelligence 108, 109, 110
intervention programme 155–63
    cognitive effects 162–3
    description 158–9
    method 156–8
    motivational effects 162, 163
    participants 156
    preliminary considerations 155–6

results 159–63
standardized mathematical assessment
    157
inverse (additive) problems 56–8, 62,
    63, **72**
    v. direct problems 56, 59–60
inverse (multiplicative) problems 119,
    119–20, *120*, 139
isomorphism of measures problems
    127–9, 130, 132, 140
    deaf *v.* hearing children 132–3

joining, related to additive reasoning
    113

key words, in story problems 15–16
Kpelle counting system 13, 14

language
    and additive composition *93*
    deaf children learning 7
    deaf children of hearing parents 7
    of mathematics 152–3
    mathematics as a form of 6–7
    and understanding of units *88*
    see also sign languages
lexical errors 105, *106*
logic 20, 21
    of additive composition 107–11
    importance of 16, 17–18
    of number system 85–6
    v. procedures 16, 17
longitudinal studies 109–10

Mann–Whitney test 160–1
matching, for counting range 34
mathematical competence 150–5
    deafness as risk factor 151, 151–2
    general processes in developing 11–20
    v. literary competence 149, 150
    scoring 3, 4
mathematical concepts
    of money 19–20, 110–11
    situations involving 19–20, 21
    theory 16–20
    of units 87–9, 90–1, 110–11
mathematical conventions 18
mathematical knowledge, informal
    of additive composition 109–10

of additive reasoning 52–3
counting 24–5, 36–7, 41, 48
deaf *v.* hearing children 24–5, 41, 48
v. formal 23–4
lack of 19–20, 154–5
of multiplication and division 112–13
of number 98–9
of sharing 123
mathematics
    attainment of deaf pupils 2–6, 20
    as a form of language 6–7
    language of 152–3
memory
    deaf *v.* hearing people 25, 153–4
    long-term 37
    reproductive *v.* reconstructive
        processes 37–8, 48
    short-term 25
memory tasks, deaf *v.* hearing children
    25–6
micro-genetic analysis 94, 95–7
mistakes, *see* errors
money
    concept of 19–20
    concept of units 110–11
    money-counting task 94
motivational effects, of intervention
    programme 162, 163
multidigit numbers 99–102, 103–4
multiplication
    age at which taught 112
    commutativity of 116–17
    direct 119, *120*
    fixed ratios 114, 119
    inverse 119, 119–20, *120*, 139
    Kpelle method 13
    with a missing factor 119–21
    as procedure 13–14
    rate *v.* ratio problems 114
    relationship between variables 114, 143
    as repeated addition 112–13
    repeated groupings 14
multiplicative reasoning 112–21, 127–48
    core of 113–27
    educational practice *v.* psychological
        research 112–13
    intervention programme 135–48
    isomorphism of measures 127–9, 130,
        132, 132–3, 140

product of measures 129–33, 140–3,
    144
representing problems 133–5
task classification 127–33
understanding of, and
    correspondences 115

NFER-Nelson tests 108, 109, 157, 158
non-verbal reasoning 10–11
number copying task 24
number labels 28, 33, 37
number lines, additive *v.* multiplicative
    reasoning 134, 143
number recall 24–8
    deaf *v.* hearing children 26
    free 26
    v. recognition 24
    serial 26, 28, 29–30, 35, 48
number representation 27
number reproduction task 24–5, 26–7
number system
    logic of 85–6
    oral, *see* counting systems
    signed, *see* counting systems
    written 85
numerical information, representation of
    60–4
numerosity 22

one-to-many correspondence 89, 90, 114
one-to-one correspondence 35–6, 101,
    113

part-whole relations 51, 77
partitive division 123, 124–6
phonological coding 25
phonological confusions 29, 30
Piaget, Jean 16, 17, 19, 24, 115
place-value system 86
    learning conventions of 97–106
preschoolers
    counting objects 35–6
    counting practice 48
    counting string 28–33, 34–5
    deaf *v.* hearing 23–36, 48
    informal *v.* formal knowledge of
        numbers 23, 24
    knowledge of numbers 23–36
    number recall 24, 26

number representation 27
number reproduction 26–7
problem solving 38–9
rule learning 25
visual coding 25
presentation, spatial *v.* sequential 25–8,
    48, 154
problem solving 36–40
    analogue representation, *see* analogue
        representation in problem solving
    children's fascination for 1–2
    through counting 38
    lack of understanding in 3
    mathematical competence and 11–16,
        20–1
    mental representation 12
    preschoolers 38–9
    procedures in 13–16
    reproductive *v.* reconstructive process
        37–8
procedures, *v.* logic 16, 17
product of measures problems 129–33,
    140–3, **144**
    deaf *v.* hearing children 132–3

quotitive division 124–6

rate *v.* ratio problems 114
ratio 128–9
    and correspondence 115
    see also fixed ratios
ratio *v.* rate problems 114
reading numbers 85, 105–6
    and additive composition 107
Realistic Mathematics Education 64
reasoning
    additive, *see* additive reasoning
    multiplicative, *see* multiplicative
        reasoning
    non-verbal 10–11
    transitive 19
    verbal 10–11
recall, *see* number recall
recognition, *v.* recall 24
reconstructive processes 37, 38, 48
regression analysis 108–9
relation between variables
    division 121, 123
    multiplication 114, 143

relational problems 116–17
repeated groupings 14
representation
    analogue, *see* analogue representation
        in problem solving
    in change problems 60–4
    in compare problems 79–81, **82, 83**
    of information 18–19
    mental 12
    of multiplicative reasoning problems
        133–5
    of numbers 27
    of numerical information 60–4
    see also signs
reproductive processes 37, 48
rule learning 25–6, 28–9, 32–3
    deaf *v.* hearing children 32–3, 48

Schonell Arithmetic Test 2–3
school placement 151–2
separating, related to additive reasoning
    113
sequence of events, representation in
    change problems 64–72
sharing 36, 121–7
    diagrams **137–8**
    direct relation 121–3
    inverse relation 121, 123–6
    see also division
Shop Task 86–8, 107–8, 110, 111
sign languages 7
    counting in 17
    rules in 32
    see also American Sign Language;
        Belgian French Sign Language;
        British Sign Language; Catalan Sign
        Language
Sign Supported English (SSE) 30, 42
signed algorithm 40–7, 49
    counting down 45
    errors in 45–6
signs (representation of numbers)
    16–17, 17, 18–19, 20, 21
situations involving mathematical con-
    cepts 19–20, 21
spatial skills 64–72, 77, 80–1, 82

spatial *v.* sequential presentation 25–8,
    48, 154
Stanford Achievement Test 4–5
story problems 15, 51, 59
    key words in 15–16
    steps in solving 12
subtraction problems 51
syntactic errors 105, *106*

tables, representing variables 128, 134,
    139–43
teaching methods 23
teaching quality, affecting deaf children's
    learning 152, 153
transformation problems 53–5
transitive inference 115
transitive reasoning 19

units (of number)
    assessing understanding of 87–9
    concept of, deaf *v.* hearing children
        87–9, 90–1
    Concept of Units Task *88*
    counting with different types of 86–8
    of different values 86
    helping understanding of 89–91

variables
    relation between, in division 121, 123
    relation between, in multiplication
        114, 143
    tables representing 128, 134, 139–43
verbal reasoning 10–11
Vergnaud, Gérard 16–17, 21, 50, 127–8
Vernon and Miller Graded Arithmetic
    Test 4
visual analogy **10**
visual coding 18, 25
vocabulary, mathematical 152–3
vocabulary knowledge 10–11

Wechsler Intelligence Scale for Children
    (WISC) 108–9
writing numbers 85, 99–106
    and additive composition 107

966344

Printed in Great Britain by
Amazon.co.uk, Ltd.,
Marston Gate.